FOR LAURA, MY VERY FAVOURITE DRINKING
AND DINING BUDDY

IZAKAYA

/ɪzəˈkʌɪə/

noun, from the Japanese izakaya 居酒屋
a type of Japanese bar in which small dishes and
snacks are served; literally: a place to stay and drink

YOUR H

FUN AND SIMPLE RECIPES INSPIRED BY THE
DRINKING-AND-DINING DENS OF JAPAN

Hardie Grant

BOOKS

HOME IZAKAYA

TIM ANDERSON

LIGHT AND FRESH
30

BOLD AND BURLY
68

DIY DINING
112

SHIME: CARBS, CARBS, CARBS
144

SWEETS
188

DRINKS
200

FUNDAMENTALS
216

PROLOGUE

At the time of writing, we are in the middle of a global pandemic that has caused the entire world to shut down. With restaurants closed, we have had to reacquaint ourselves with home cooking. For some, this has presented itself primarily as a chore or an annoyance – especially the washing up. But for me, this has been an almost unconditional joy. I have relished the simplicity of home cooking and the freedom of it: the permission to cook creatively and earnestly without having to worry about paying customers. I have cooked things I have always loved cooking, and I have cooked things I love eating but never have had the time to cook, and I have cooked things I have never cooked before.

Since we cannot travel, I have also turned to cooking as a form of escapism. Of course you can't actually, physically, transport yourself to a night market in Chiang Mai when you eat *khao soi,* any more than Proust could reverse the ageing process or travel through time when he ate a madeleine. But you can get somewhere, mentally, through food, and the journey can be profound. I made *carnitas tacos* that put me, for a moment, in a squarely Los Angeles state of mind. I barbecued rabbit and drank Kinnie to take me back to Malta, a year after we went on holiday there. I made a proper deep-dish Chicago-style pizza on the day we were supposed to fly back to the Midwest. And I made garlicky prawn wontons, slicked with chilli oil, to bring me to my favourite Sichuanese restaurants, peppered throughout London's Docklands: a region now so inaccessible, it may as well have been in China itself.

Of course, it doesn't always work. You can't really recreate the effect of eating certain things in the setting where they're meant to be eaten, and my post-lockdown to-do list contains exactly these types of context-dependent food experience: the chopsticks-on-ceramic clamour of a busy dim sum dining room; the plutocratic, red wine-and-bearnaise-sodden excess of a steakhouse; the carnival of smoke, sugar, *soju* and spice that is a Korean barbecue joint. There are some things that you can't quite do justice to at home.

This included, I thought, my very favourite type of place to eat: **izakaya**. I'd always figured that izakaya are too dependent on their intangible characteristics to successfully recreate at home. They're about the service, the atmosphere and, crucially, the ability to have an effortless time because somebody else is putting in the effort. You do not have to worry about dirty dishes in an izakaya. That's not part of the deal. There are no toddlers to look after in an izakaya. There are no worries at all: the izakaya is a stress-free zone. How can you achieve this without physically relocating to that 'third space' separate from your workplace and your home? Indeed, how can you achieve this without actually going to Japan? It seemed impossible.

But then I remembered Bar Yuki.

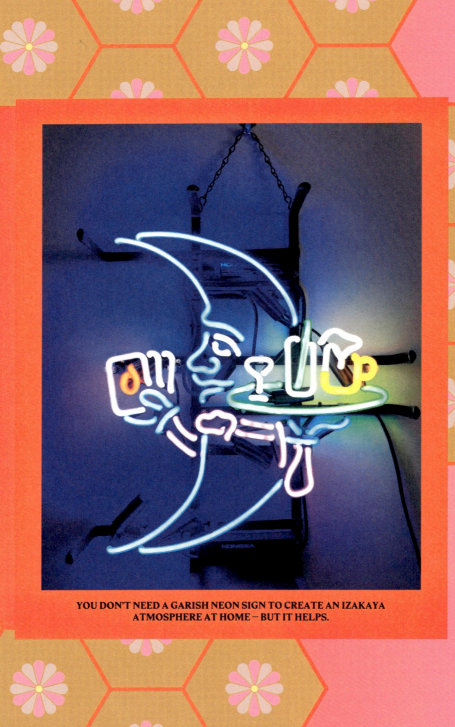

YOU DON'T NEED A GARISH NEON SIGN TO CREATE AN IZAKAYA
ATMOSPHERE AT HOME – BUT IT HELPS.

BAR YUKI
IS OPEN

In preparing to write this book, I began reminiscing about the best izakaya experiences I've ever had. There have been so many, but to be honest, my specific memories of most of them are quite hazy, blurred by alcohol and age-related brain degeneration. But one izakaya did stand out in my mind as an all-time favourite: Bar Yuki. I was trying to think of really good izakaya here in London and, unfortunately, there are not very many at all. This isn't the fault of chefs or restaurateurs in particular; it's just that izakaya work better in Japan, for all kinds of reasons. But I was still startled by the realisation that my favourite izakaya in London isn't an actual restaurant. It's my friend Yuki's flat, in Limehouse.

What makes 'Bar Yuki', as she calls it, so good? Well, first of all, Yuki is a very good cook. Very, *annoyingly* good. When I think of chefs I look up to, she's always at the top of the list. Yuki was born and raised in the south of Japan, and she has been cooking her entire life; by the age of five, she was already helping her mother with odd jobs in the kitchen, including, most impressively, gutting fish. Yuki credits her mother and grandparents for teaching her how to cook, and not just basic Japanese home cooking. Apparently, if Yuki said she liked something at a restaurant while she was out with her family, her mother would try to figure out what was in it and then recreate it at home. This is something Yuki now does as well, and because she's a studious, serious cook, pretty much everything she turns her hand to is enviably delicious.

But it's not just her food that impresses; it's also her generosity. Even when I pop in unexpectedly, Yuki will lay out a platter of charcuterie or fry up some gyoza from the freezer. Perhaps too much is made of *omotenashi*, Japan's culture of superlative hospitality, but it is one of those clichés that does tend to be true more often than not.

I asked Yuki if her family also instilled in her a sense of obligation to serve house guests, and she explained that it's a bit more complicated than that. First of all, there is a cultural expectation in Japan that you should offer something to people in your home, but also a reciprocal expectation that they'll bring something for you. This give-and-take is so ingrained in Japanese society that it simply feels natural to provide a little something for visitors. As for omotenashi, Yuki explains that in friends' homes or in izakaya, it's the same spirit of hospitality you'd find in more formal settings but expressed in a friendlier, more laid-back way. 'Izakaya are like pubs,' she says, contrasting them with high-end cocktail bars; the experience and the service are basically the same, but 'the communication with the person behind the bar is different'.

Additionally, Yuki says it just seems wrong to see people drinking without food – like there's something missing. She confesses to being a lightweight who can't really drink without eating, so sometimes she makes food simply as a means of self-preservation, and I get to reap the benefits. 'I tend to make something because *I* want to have it!' she says with a laugh. But she also says that the impulse to serve food when people are drinking is automatic, because that's what she's always known – it's the norm in Japan. When she said this, it did occur to

me that I could hardly think of any situations in Japan where people were drinking and not eating something along with it; even at really casual bars that didn't serve food, you'd at least be given a little bowl of nuts or rice crackers, free of charge. Convenience stores even sell cans of beer with little packets of snacks attached directly to them. Spend enough time in Japan and you'll develop a sense that drinking just doesn't feel right without something to nibble on. 'I think drinking with snacks is just in our genes, in our blood,' Yuki explains. She says that making a good home izakaya may actually be as simple as having 'small bits you can always serve' on hand, like ham, pickles or cheese – just a little something to make your guests, or yourself, feel more nourished and provided for.

Of course, I mustn't neglect to mention another key player in Bar Yuki's enduring charm: Yuki's partner, Luke. Luke is not Japanese. Luke's as white as mayonnaise, as British as a wedge of Wensleydale. And yet it's Luke who really sets the tone at Bar Yuki. The political journalist Dahlia Lithwick once wrote that there are two types of people in the world: Order Muppets and Chaos Muppets. You may already be able to guess which category Luke and Yuki fall under. Yuki is, generally speaking, no nonsense. Luke is something approaching *all* nonsense. Luke's got a zesty sense of humour and a cabinet full of fine spirits, and he's generous with both. When I asked Luke what he brings to the Bar Yuki experience, he simply replied, '*Electric frisson*', then cackled like a lunatic.

Some years ago, Luke bought a neon sign. This particular neon sign is just about as far beyond the boundaries of good taste as

something can be. It's bright blue and yellow, in the shape of an anthropomorphic crescent moon, carrying a tray of drinks in one hand and a deck of cards in the other. It is one of the silliest objects I have ever laid eyes on. It is also undeniably, and crucially, *fun*. Plus, it's conversational; the first time you see it, it's hard not to comment on it. These are all things a good izakaya should be: light-hearted, atmospheric and conducive to inane chatter.

We can't all have a Luke and Yuki, or a ludicrous neon sign. But clearly, Bar Yuki goes to show that we *can* have a great izakaya experience at home. All you need is some good food, good company and a few choice Japanese drinks to enhance both.

All of these things are achievable.

YUKI, ENJOYING A DRINK, BUT PROBABLY
THINKING ABOUT FOOD.

ON OMOTENASHI

Omotenashi is a Japanese concept often described as a way of anticipating and fulfilling guests' needs before they're even expressed. To me, omotenashi makes you feel genuinely cared for in a holistic way; it's not just slavish formality, it's a sense of being looked after. There are some in Japan who quite reasonably find keeping up the politesse of omotenashi culture tedious or oppressive, for customers and workers alike; 'the customer is god' is a phrase used to describe omotenashi as both a positive and a negative. In his 'defense of omotenashi' in *Metropolis* magazine, Masaru Urano explains:

It's very easy to conflate omotenashi *with the politeness forced as a result of the 'customer is god' consumer culture. However, I think that true* omotenashi *lies elsewhere. Omotenashi, or a purer version of it, is alive and well in the local* shokudos *(casual restaurants), mom-and-pop grocery stores and small* ryokans *(inns) hidden deep in the countryside. The same* irasshaimase *[welcome] can be heard, but it's a less forced, more genuine type of* irasshaimase. *They're the sort of places where customers can strike up conversations with the clerks and exchange gossip about the neighbourhood. They're the sort of places where the* keigo *(honorific language) is more conversational, where the elderly couple running the shop treats you more like a treasured grandchild than a 'god'.*

I generally agree, but I would say that true omotenashi actually *can* be found in big cities and convenience stores. My wife Laura often talks fondly of her 'Lawson lady', an older worker at her local *conbini* (convenience store), Lawson, who wasn't just friendly and polite, but genuinely warm and caring. She would engage Laura in conversation and give her extra fried chicken for free when she came in for lunch, and when Laura said she was leaving Japan to return to the UK, the Lawson lady actually wept. How sweet is that?

Urano's praise of a more casual, heartfelt omotenashi spirit is absolutely true, I think – and this sounds to me more like the kind of hospitality you receive in an izakaya or, perhaps more to the point, in someone's home. The great Spanish chef José Pizarro once told me that he thinks of his restaurant as his house, and his customers as his friends. This is a lovely sentiment – but it begs the question: if someone's home is the benchmark for good hospitality, then maybe that just goes to show homes are inherently more generous, jovial places to eat? It didn't take me long after opening my own restaurant to realise that true hospitality is corrupted somewhat whenever money changes hands.

WARNING: CONTAINS FUSION!

Many of the recipes in this book might be described as fusion food: Japanese dishes remixed with global flavours or vice-versa. Some dishes, such as Wafu Fondue (page 125) or Korean-style Beef Tartare (page 80), aren't Japanese at all. So you may justifiably wonder why they're in a Japanese cookbook. The answer is that these are things that actually can be found on izakaya menus in Japan, because they're fun and good with booze, and that's what I'm trying to capture in this book: not just traditional Japanese dishes, but a whole way of Japanese dining, the sense of welcoming and letting loose that are hallmarks of izakaya culture.

My perception of Japanese food culture is in line with that of the historian Eric Rath, who proposes that we should adopt the term 'Japan's cuisines' as opposed to 'Japanese cuisine'. This is a subtle but important distinction that highlights the real diversity of Japanese gastronomy. Japanese food has many threads, and often these threads interweave with other cultures in wonderful, fascinating, delicious ways. That so many people still seem to think of Japanese culture as somehow monolithic and insular irks me no end. In general, I have found Japanese people to be quite generous in sharing their own culture, and open-minded when it comes to the culture of others. In fact, many of Japan's most beloved dishes started off as a kind of fusion, with not very distant origins in other countries' cuisines.

Anyway, it's almost a cliché at this point to say that all food is some sort of fusion, but I feel I should disclaim that you should be aware – as I am – that a lot of these recipes are not 100% Japanese. But they are 100% izakaya.

I——ZAKA——YA

居

酒

屋

TO STAY—SAKE—SHOP

INTRODUCTION

Izakaya are sometimes described as 'Japanese tapas bars'. This is a little misleading because it sort of suggests that izakaya are a Japanese interpretation of Spanish-style dining, and it also implies that izakaya dishes are quite small, which is not always the case. That said, I think the translation is pretty apt, primarily because both izakaya and tapas bars are centred on drinking. In fact, izakaya began as sake shops that allowed customers to drink on the premises, later introducing snacks and small dishes (called *otsumami* or *sake no sakana*) that would encourage people to stay and drink more. Like most of the world's great drinking foods, these dishes tend to be strongly flavoured and addictive. I'm a big, dumb American with a big, dumb American palate, which is probably why this is my favourite genre of Japanese food; it appeals to my natural predisposition to cover everything in melted cheese and hot sauce. (Indeed, izakaya meals can actually involve a surprisingly large amount of cheese.)

But while izakaya food does, on the whole, skew in the direction of the spicy, salty, meaty and deep-fried, it doesn't always, and I think really good izakaya meals have the same sort of satisfying balance found in many other modes of Japanese dining. In fact, izakaya food is kind of difficult to pin down, because it is quite broad and all-encompassing; in some ways, it represents the whole of Japanese gastronomy in microcosm – and then some. Izakaya menus are not limited to Japanese cuisine, often incorporating drinking food from around the world. Many izakaya take an 'anything goes' approach to what they serve; as long as it's fun and tastes good with beer or sake, it's fair game.

I often tell people about one of my favourite izakaya in Kitakyushu, the city where I lived in Japan. Their offering was pretty much entirely traditional Japanese food, with all of the usual suspects like sashimi and tempura, but they also offered fondue (see my version on page 125). Not even with a Japanese twist or anything – just straight up Swiss cheese fondue. (Come to think of it, I just remembered an 'Irish' pub in Kitakyushu that also served fondue. They served blowfish and chips, too. That place was awesome.) But hey, why not? If there's a heaven, surely it is filled with hot cheese and cold sake.

15

IZAKAYA:
A HOW-TO GUIDE

SO, HOW EXACTLY DO YOU SERVE AN IZAKAYA MEAL?
HERE IS A STEP-BY-STEP PROCESS:

1
Get a bottle of sake
(or two) in the fridge.

2
Cook some food –
a pot of rice and two or three
other things ought to do it.

3
Dim the lights down to somewhere
between 'romantic' and 'I can't see my
food'. If you have a red paper lantern
to hand, hang it in a corner of the
room and switch it on.

4
Ask a neighbour to stand outside
your window and smoke cigarettes so
you get a bit of second-hand smoke
wafting in. (Please don't actually
do this; it's bad for you and your
neighbour, and you can't smoke in
most izakaya in Japan anymore,
so it's not even accurate.)

5
Summon at least one other
person to the dining table.

6
Lay the food out artfully.
Bask in your guests' admiration
and gratitude.

7
Take turns pouring sake for each
other in between mouthfuls of the
delicious food you've made, while
nodding happily and saying 'oishii!'

8
Repeat step 7 until you
have achieved transcendence.

This is how you might serve an
izakaya meal if you're really going all
in. And indeed, drinks, atmosphere
and etiquette and all that certainly
make a difference if you're trying to
impress, but this book is intended
to be something you can easily cook
from on a regular basis, so you can
create chilled-out izakaya vibes even
on a weeknight. And for that, all
you'll really need is this:

GOOD
FOOD

GOOD
COMPANY
(EVEN IF IT'S JUST YOURSELF
OR YOUR PET)

GOOD
DRINKS
(PAGES 200–215)

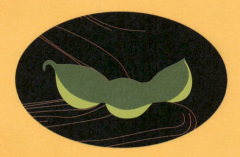

The food is key, of course. Most Japanese meals are all about variety and balance, so ideally they'll consist of a few different things. Much of this book is categorised into two sections: 'Light and Fresh' and 'Bold and Burly'. Generally speaking, a fine meal can be made by choosing one from each section, plus a serving of rice or something from the chapter on Shime (page 144): literally a 'tying off' course, big and carby and satisfying. If you don't cook Japanese food often at home, it can be tricky to know how much to prepare, so at the bottom of each recipe, I've suggested meal plans for two people; simply scale the recipes up (almost all of them scale perfectly well) as needed for more people or, better yet, add another couple of dishes if you have time.

A guiding principle often cited when discussing Japanese meal plans is *ichijū sansai*, meaning 'one soup, three sides'. However, this is a little misleading because that doesn't include rice or pickles, which are prerequisite, and because the 'three sides' in this format can vary widely in size. Also, izakaya meals aren't usually anchored to traditional formats like this. But one particularly useful takeaway from ichijū sansai is that rice and pickles are a great place to start – add to these just one or two other recipes from this book, perhaps with a salad or miso soup (bagged salads and instant miso soup are fine!) and you'll be looking at a really good meal.

But feel free to play around and have fun with the way you serve these dishes. Mix and match them as you like, and bear in mind that if you make too much, most of the recipes will make fine leftovers. Of course, to cook Japanese food at home, you will need Japanese ingredients. So stock up!

KEY TERMS

THESE ARE A FEW IZAKAYA VOCABULARY WORDS THAT ARE WORTH FAMILIARISING YOURSELF WITH, AS THEY WILL COME UP FREQUENTLY IN THIS BOOK, AND IN IZAKAYA DISCOURSE GENERALLY.

B-KYŪ GURUME

Literally 'B-grade gourmet', this is a term of endearment bestowed upon humbler, cheaper Japanese fare such as curry rice, beef bowls, ramen and yakitori. This genre of cooking overlaps heavily with izakaya food.

CHŪKA RYŌRI

This refers to Japanese-Chinese food, which is quite nebulous and doesn't always actually originate in China, in much the same way that chop suey or General Tso's chicken are called 'Chinese' in the US. Chūka dishes are typically characterised by a generous use of strongly flavoured ingredients like sesame oil, ginger, garlic and chilli.

OMOTENASHI

A Japanese mode of hospitality in which guests are made to feel truly looked after; this can be expressed in both formal and casual ways, so long as an underlying spirit of generosity and care is conveyed. (See page 12 for more of an explanation.)

OTSUMAMI AND SAKANA

These two terms refer to drinking food; otsumami means 'snacks', but it literally means 'to pick', with an honorific prefix. Students of Japanese language learn early on that sakana means 'fish', but this usage is relatively recent. The original meaning of sakana was, in fact, food to have with sake; literally, 'sake vegetables'. Over time, it became more common to serve fish and seafood with sake, and so the word sakana became synonymous with fish. In an izakaya context, sakana and otsumami are more or less interchangeable, but if a distinction is to be made between them, it is that otsumami are perhaps better for beer, whereas sakana are better for sake.

SHIME

Shime means 'tie up', and it is a 'tying-off' course at the end of an izakaya meal, typically large, carb-heavy and satisfying. For the purposes of home cooking, shime (which are in their own chapter on page 144) can generally be prepared as a meal in and of themselves.

YŌSHOKU

This is Japan's original fusion food, literally 'Western food', although most of it would not be recognised as such in the actual West. It is essentially a catch-all term for dishes with origins outside of Japan or China, however distant they may be; it includes many iconic dishes such as okonomiyaki, curry rice, croquettes and gratins. It is hearty, flavourful stuff, which makes it ideal for izakaya menus.

ESSENTIAL IZAKAYA INGREDIENTS

There are seven essential Japanese ingredients you should always have on hand, since they're so common and fundamental in Japanese recipes: **soy sauce, rice vinegar, miso, sake, mirin, Japanese rice**, and some form of **dashi**. When it comes to soy sauce and rice vinegar, there are many varieties, but the main thing is to make sure you are buying Japanese ones rather than continental Asian versions, as they taste remarkably different. The soy sauce used for every recipe in this book is *shōyu* – basic, all-purpose Japanese soy sauce. Miso is broadly divided into white and red varieties, a distinction based primarily on age; white miso is younger and has a lighter flavour, while red miso is older, richer and more aromatic. In most cases, either one will do, but I've indicated in each recipe if you should use one rather than the other.

Sake can be actual 'cooking sake' or just any old plonk; it's a bit of a waste to use pricy premium sake in food (see page 203 for drinking sake). The related mirin – sort of like a sweet sake syrup – falls into two main price brackets, *hon-mirin* ('true mirin') and 'mirin-style seasoning,' which are determined by production methods and alcohol content. Hon-mirin certainly has more character and fragrance, but the cheap stuff is absolutely fine for everyday home cooking. As for Japanese rice, it's often labelled 'sushi rice' here in the UK, which is weird, because sushi rice is rice that's been cooked and seasoned a certain way, not a variety of rice, but anyway, that's what you should look out for. Dashi is an absolutely essential flavour in Japanese cuisine; it is a light yet flavourful broth made from dried kelp and fish. You can make it from scratch (page 220), but I would highly recommend buying instant **dashi powder**, which is cheap, delicious, and in no way inauthentic or a 'cheat', if that is a concern.

These ingredients are so common and useful that you should have them in your cupboard at all times.

MORE IZAKAYA INGREDIENTS

The above ingredients are so ubiquitous in Japanese recipes (and useful for other kinds of cooking) that it's a good idea to always have them on hand. The following are also common, but you'll only need them for specific recipes.

CHICKEN STOCK POWDER AND MSG

Here, I'm talking about Japanese or Chinese chicken stock powder, which differs significantly from stock cubes in a few key respects. First, it contains a higher concentration of powdered chicken fat, which gives it a slick mouthfeel and stronger, meatier chicken flavour. It is also more garlicky and gingery and less herby than European stock cubes, and it contains the umami compounds inosinate and guanylate, which give it a huge, satisfying savouriness. It's fantastic stuff.

Some other recipes here call for MSG, used to a similar effect. I find it indispensable not just for Japanese food but for pretty much all food. In response to any of the purported 'risks': MSG is completely safe and occurs naturally in thousands of traditional foods, including cheese, miso, bacon, anchovies and Marmite. You are already eating it, whether you want to or not, and there is no difference between naturally occurring MSG and manufactured MSG. So-called 'Chinese restaurant syndrome' is not real, and what's more, it's racist slander.

Chicken stock powder comes in tins that are almost always yellow with a red or green lid. MSG can be found in cute little shakers with a panda face on them, but I buy it in big half-kilo sacks. Ajinomoto is a decent brand for both.

DAIKON

Daikon are huge white radishes, used not only in Japan but across much of Asia. They taste very similar to European radishes but they're less tedious to prep because they're so large. In the UK, daikon are often sold as 'mooli', which is the Urdu word for them. Choose daikon that are firm and heavy, not floppy or soft.

JAPANESE BROWN SAUCE AND JAPANESE MAYO

Japanese brown sauce has many variants, such as tonkatsu sauce, yakisoba sauce, okonomiyaki sauce and takoyaki sauce. They all fall under the category of what's simply called 'sauce' in Japan, as they have similar flavours, with slight variations in terms of consistency and balance. Tonkatsu sauce is a good choice if you need something that will work well in a variety of recipes. You can make it at home but I would strongly recommend buying it. The same goes for Japanese mayo, known for its creamier, eggier, deliciously MSG-enhanced flavour. The brand Kewpie seems to be everywhere these days, and while it is expensive, it's worth it. Normal mayo just doesn't cut it.

JAPANESE PICKLES

If you have rice and pickles, you have the foundation of a Japanese dinner, so they're always good to have on hand. You can make your own – see Shiozuke Pickles and Quick Pickle Brine (both page 224).

TOASTED SESAME OIL

Sesame oil adds a thumping bass note to harmonise with treble clef flavours like ponzu and rice vinegar. Unlike soy sauce or rice vinegar, there's no need to get a Japanese one. Chinese sesame oil is basically the same, and in fact this is often used to give a so-called 'Chinese' flavour to izakaya dishes.

KOMBU AND KATSUOBUSHI

These are dried kelp and dried, smoked tuna flakes, respectvely. They are the primary ingredients for making dashi, a key skill to learn that also yields some delicious by-products (page 221). Buying good-quality kombu will make a big difference to the flavour of your dashi, and as for katsuobushi, make sure to check its best-by date. Old katsuobushi can develop an ammonia-like smell, which is not nice. Fresh is best.

NORI AND AONORI

These tasty seaweed products are subtle but important garnishes for a wide variety of Japanese dishes, both traditional and modern. Nori is usually sold as sheets, for making sushi rolls, but in this book it is used mainly in a shredded form, called *kizami* nori. You can buy pre-shredded nori like this at Asian supermarkets but it's also easy to shred nori sheets yourself with sharp kitchen shears. Aonori is a different species from nori, but with a similar flavour, and it is sold as little flakes.

PANKO

Japanese breadcrumbs, called panko, are superior to their European counterparts, with a lighter, crunchier texture. All supermarkets sell panko now, but most supermarket brands are very poor; the panko is way too chunky. Buy a Japanese brand, and from an Asian supermarket, if you can.

PONZU

Ponzu, or more accurately *ponzu-jōyu*, is a thin sauce made primarily from citrus juice and soy sauce. It is extremely delicious and versatile, and there are now some good bottled versions available – I particularly like the *sudachi* ponzu sold by the Wasabi Company here in the UK. However, it is also easy to make yourself (page 222), and it will have more aroma if you use freshly squeezed citrus.

RAMEN OR CHINESE-STYLE WHEAT NOODLES

Japan's got many kinds of noodles, of course, but in this book only one comes up more than once: *chūka-men* or Chinese wheat noodles. Most Anglophones will know these as egg noodles, but they don't always contain egg; they're similar to ramen, and good ones contain the alkaline salts potassium carbonate and/or sodium carbonate to give them a firm, bouncy texture. These ingredients are often indicated only by their E numbers, E500 and E501. Either fresh or dried noodles are fine.

RED PICKLED GINGER

The vast majority of pickled ginger sold in the UK is *gari*, the thinly sliced, pink or pale yellow ginger in a sweet brine used almost exclusively as a garnish for sushi. This is annoying because the more versatile variety of pickled ginger is *beni shōga*, which is red, julienned and less sweet, and used in dozens of classic Japanese dishes. Seek this out – it is available online or at Asian supermarkets.

SHICHIMI, CHILLI OIL AND DRIED CHILLIES

Shichimi, or more fully *shichimi tōgarashi*, is one of Japan's most ubiquitous seasonings – a blend of chilli powder and six other aromatic ingredients, such as orange zest and ginger. Chilli oil is another popular choice for adding heat and aroma to dishes, found in many izakaya preparations. Chinese or Japanese varieties are vastly preferable to European ones, which is to say: please don't use European chilli oils. Chilli oils with 'bits' in them are always good, but Chinese or other continental Asian ones may contain jarringly non-Japanese ingredients, like fermented black beans, so it's best to get a Japanese one if you can. A few other recipes call for dried red chillies; these are the moderately hot Chinese chillies sold at any Asian grocer, blood red in colour and about 5 cm (2 in) long.

YUZU

Yuzu is a wonderfully aromatic Japanese citrus fruit, and while you can occasionally purchase fresh ones outside of Japan, you're more likely to encounter its bottled juice. It does tend to be expensive, but don't be tempted by cheap yuzu juice blends – they lack the aroma of pure yuzu, so they don't actually offer good value for money.

TOFU

There are two main types of tofu used in Japanese cooking: cotton (*momen*) and silken (*kinugoshi*), which refers to their texture. Cotton has a harder, more crumbly consistency, whereas silken is, well, silken – smooth and delicate. Cotton tofu is often not labelled as such, since it seems to be the default tofu in the UK, and it is sold refrigerated, floating in its whey. Silken tofu is sold ambient, in Tetrapaks. They are not interchangeable because of how they behave during various cooking processes; I've indicated which to buy in each recipe, so make sure you get the right one.

TOASTED SESAME SEEDS

Repeat after me: I WILL NOT USE UNTOASTED SESAME SEEDS IN JAPANESE FOOD, SO HELP ME GOD. This is one of my biggest peeves. Sesame seeds are invariably consumed toasted in Japan; they're so much more flavourful than the un-toasted version that I don't even understand why they're sold that way. You can buy toasted sesame seeds at Asian supermarkets but it's cheaper to buy raw sesame seeds and toast them yourself. Do this in a dry frying pan (skillet) set over a medium heat, tossing frequently until golden brown.

TSUYU

Tsuyu is essentially a concentrated, highly seasoned dashi that can be used as a dip or sauce on its own, or diluted with hot water to make a tasty broth for noodles and other dishes. Tsuyu is easy to make (page 220) but the bottled stuff is very tasty and can't be beaten for convenience.

WASABI

You can now buy fresh wasabi easily online, and it is *such* a treat – it is expensive, but a little goes a long way, and is simply in another league compared to the stuff that comes in a tube. In fact, the tubed stuff is often made from a mixture of wasabi and horseradish, dyed green. It's fine, of course, but if you're making sashimi with lovely, top-quality fish, I feel it deserves some lovely, top-quality wasabi. If you buy fresh wasabi you should also buy a wasabi grater, which will turn it into a beautiful, airy mash – standard graters, even microplanes, won't work.

RECIPE NOTES

1 tablespoon is 15 ml.

1 teaspoon is 5 ml.

Dashi
indicates prepared liquid dashi.

Dashi powder
indicates the powder itself.

Deep-frying
Check the guide on page 99.

Measure by volume or weight
as the recipe indicates.

Quantities for rice and noodles
are provided as 'portions' rather than
as specific weights, so you can use your own
judgement based on your own hunger. But as
a general guide, one portion of rice is 75–100 g
(2½–3½ oz/½ cup) uncooked weight, and one
portion of noodles is 150 g (5 oz) if they are
fresh, or 100 g (3½ oz) if they are dried.

Oil
indicates neutral vegetable oil.

Rice
must be Japanese, Korean or
Taiwanese short-grain rice.

Sesame oil and **sesame seeds**
must always be toasted.

Soy sauce
must be Japanese soy sauce
and not tamari.

Sugar
indicates white caster (superfine)
or granulated sugar.

Use fine salt
unless sea salt flakes are specified.

Use fresh ingredients
unless frozen, dried or tinned are specified.

Vinegar
indicates Japanese rice vinegar.

Izakaya are so good at what they do, they've even developed *salads* that make for great drinking food. This section contains dishes that are light and refreshing, often vegetable-based and/or served cold. But many of them still have strong, zingy flavours with sharp seasonings like ponzu and chilli.

爽やかで軽めの料理

LIGHT & FRESH

FIRST OF ALL, EDAMAME

とりあえず、枝豆

TORIAEZU, EDAMAME

Over the years, I've done all kinds of things to edamame in misguided attempts to make them more 'interesting'. While many of these variations have been pretty good, I'm not sure any of them have actually been an improvement on plain, boiled edamame. I've come to realise that eating edamame ought to be a mellow and mindless experience, something pleasantly bland to munch on in between sips of beer while you unburden yourself of the stresses of the day just passed. Edamame are meditation, in bean form.

Of course, edamame should also be addictive, like a bowl of nuts – and the simplest way to achieve this is with our old friends salt, sugar and MSG.

SERVES 2–4 AS A SNACK BEFORE A MEAL

500 ml (17 fl oz/2 cups) water
3 tbsp soy sauce
1 tsp fine salt
200–250 g (7–9 oz) frozen edamame
2 large pinches of sea salt
1–2 pinches of MSG
1 tsp sugar

METHOD

Bring the water to the boil in a saucepan over a medium-high heat and add the soy sauce and fine salt. Once the salt has dissolved and the liquid has come back to a rolling boil, lower in the edamame. Let the liquid come back to the boil, then cook for another 3–4 minutes. Drain, then toss with the sea salt, MSG and sugar. Serve in a bowl with a small dish on top of it to keep them nice and hot; keep the dish on the table for discarded pods.

MEAL FOR TWO WITH

This is sort of a light pre-dinner snack rather than something that forms part of a meal – so find another recipe and go from there!

PAIR WITH

Anything! But something quaffable like beer, highballs or iced green tea are all ideal.

ADDICTIVE CABBAGE

やみつきキャベツ

YAMITSUKI KYABETSU

At many izakaya and similar informal restaurants in Japan, when you sit down you'll be given a little plate of chopped cabbage, dressed in a tangy sauce that makes it irresistibly delicious. I didn't learn until after I left Japan that this little freebie is called *yamitsuki kyabetsu*, which means 'addictive cabbage', and it does indeed sit up there with edamame in the rankings of simple but effective veg-based beer fodder.

SERVES 2–4

½ garlic clove, minced or finely grated
1 tbsp sesame oil
1 tbsp vinegar
1 tbsp soy sauce
1 tbsp sesame seeds, crushed
1 tsp chicken stock powder (optional)
½ sweetheart (hispi) cabbage, core removed and roughly chopped
freshly ground black pepper (optional)

METHOD

Combine the garlic and all the seasonings, except the black pepper, in a large plastic bag, then add the cabbage. Seal the bag and shake it well, then empty the contents onto a serving dish. Garnish with the black pepper, if using.

MEAL FOR TWO WITH

Karaage 6.0 (page 104), rice and pickles.

PAIR WITH

Beer (particularly lager), table sake or iced green tea.

RADISH AND WATERCRESS SALAD

ラディッシュとクレソンのサラダ RADDISHU TO KURESON NO SARADA

Most of the time, salad is existentially dull. Too often when I eat salad, I can't help but think, 'What is the point of this? What does it all *mean?!*' and I spend the rest of the evening in a deep depression. My reaction to bad salads has ruined many dates. But not so with izakaya salads, which are delightful and invigorating, festive with colour and crunch and moreish, tangy dressings. This salad would ordinarily be made with daikon and mizuna (a mild but very crunchy salad leaf in the mustard family) and those would be ideal, if you can source them. Otherwise, the more readily available radishes and watercress are more than adequate substitutes; in fact, I love the extra colour and subtle bitterness they provide. Regardless of which you use, you're in for a truly non-depressing salad.

METHOD

If using the *shirasu*, pour the oil into a frying pan and set over a medium heat. Add the shirasu and stir-fry for about 5 minutes until light golden brown. Remove from the oil and drain on paper towels. Grate or julienne the radishes, then pile them on top of the watercress in a serving dish. If making the alternative dressing, mix all the ingredients together in a small bowl. Pour over your chosen dressing, then use scissors to snip the nori into very thin shreds on top of the salad. Garnish with the crispy shirasu, if using.

SERVES 2–4

1 tbsp oil (optional)
15 g (½ oz) *shirasu* (baby anchovies) (optional); crispy fried onions are an excellent substitute
250 g (9 oz) radishes (watermelon radishes are ideal if you can get them)
50–60 g (2 oz) watercress, mizuna or other flavourful, crunchy greens
¼ sheet of nori
5–6 tbsp Wafu Dressing (page 222)

OR THE FOLLOWING DRESSING:

2 tbsp vinegar
2 tbsp soy sauce
½ tbsp sugar
1 tsp lemon juice
¼ tsp dashi powder or MSG

TIP

This recipe calls for shirasu, which are itty-bitty baby fish. Real Japanese shirasu are very hard to find indeed, but you can get the Korean equivalent in the fridge or freezer section of most Asian supermarkets, usually labelled 'baby anchovies'. But if you can't get them at all, don't worry – the salad will still be delicious without them, or you can replace them with crispy fried onions.

MEAL FOR TWO WITH
Wafu Fondue (page 125).

PAIR WITH
Sake (any kind, really), dry white wine or iced barley tea.

SWEET CHILLI MAYO PRAWNS

スイートチリ海老マヨ SUĪTO CHIRI EBI MAYO

SERVES 2

200–250 g (7–9 oz) raw king prawns (shrimp), shelled and deveined
1 tsp sake
1 pinch of white pepper
1 tsp soy sauce
4 tbsp potato starch or cornflour (cornstarch)
2 tbsp sweet chilli sauce
2 tbsp mayonnaise
oil, for shallow frying
shichimi, as needed (optional)
1 handful of lettuce or other crisp salad leaves (optional)
¼ lemon

I always think of this as a quintessential izakaya dish, but it isn't actually that common. In fact, I think I've only had it at izakaya a couple of times, but it is utterly perfect drinking food: snacky, crispy, savoury, a little bit spicy and a little bit sweet. It's almost like something that might be served at an American sports bar. Is it even Japanese? I don't know, but it is 100% izakaya and 100% delicious.

METHOD

Toss the prawns with the sake, white pepper, half the soy sauce and 1 tbsp of the potato starch or cornflour until evenly coated. Combine the remaining soy sauce with the sweet chilli sauce and mayo in a large bowl and stir until evenly mixed. Pour the oil into a deep pan to a depth of about 2.5 cm (1 in) and place over a high heat. Test the oil temperature by dripping a few drops of the prawn batter into it; it's hot enough when the batter sizzles and floats immediately. Dredge the prawns in the remaining potato starch, then lower them into the oil carefully, one by one, so they don't stick together. Fry them for about 4 minutes until golden brown, turning them a few times while cooking. Remove the prawns with a slotted spoon and drain on paper towels. Leave to cool for a few minutes, then toss through the sweet chilli mayo. To serve, lay some salad leaves on a plate (if using), place the prawns on top, then garnish with the shichimi, if using. Serve with the lemon wedge on the side.

MEAL FOR TWO WITH

Glass Noodle and Cucumber Salad (page 38) and maybe some rice or Furikake Potatoes (page 100).

PAIR WITH

Fruity, off-dry white wine, lager or iced oolong tea.

GLASS NOODLE AND CUCUMBER SALAD

きゅうりと春雨の中華サラダ KYŪRI TO HARUSAME NO CHŪKA SARADA

I love an evocative noodle name. The Italians are good at this, with their radiatore, farfalle, vermicelli and, my favourite, strozzapreti: 'priest-chokers'. Then there is Korean *olchaengi guksu* ('tadpole noodles'), Cantonese *cheung fun* ('intestine noodles') and German spätzle ('little sparrows'). That last one is just adorable. For their part, the Japanese have a few, but the most poetic must be *harusame*: 'spring rain'. Harusame are glass or cellophane noodles (also quite evocative names, it must be said), which are not that common in Japan, and therefore salads such as this that include them are often listed on menus as 'Chinese style' salads. I don't know how Chinese they really are, but they're really good; the noodles carry sauce wonderfully, and they make the salad a bit more substantial without being heavy.

METHOD

Place the noodles in a bowl and cover them with just-boiled water. Leave to rehydrate for 5 minutes, then rinse under cold water until well chilled. Squeeze out the noodles, then transfer to a mixing bowl. If you are using kombu, cut it into wide strips, about 4 cm (1½ in) across, then slice the strips into very fine shreds. Toss the noodles together with all the remaining ingredients until everything is well mixed and well coated.

SERVES 2–4

40 g (1½ oz) glass noodles
rehydrated kombu from making dashi (page 220) (optional)
1 cucumber, julienned
1 small-ish carrot, grated or julienned
50 g (2 oz) ham, cooked chicken or firm cotton tofu, cut into bite-size pieces
1 tbsp sesame seeds, crushed to the consistency of coarse sand
2 tbsp vinegar
2 tbsp soy sauce
½ tbsp sugar
½ tbsp lemon or yuzu juice
1 tsp sesame oil
¼ tsp dashi powder or MSG

MEAL FOR TWO WITH

Sweet Chilli Mayo Prawns (page 37) and perhaps some rice.

PAIR WITH

Shōchū, on the rocks or as a highball. Sake, beer or iced tea are good, too.

TIP

This recipe uses kombu from making dashi, but it'll still be really tasty without it, so if you've not made dashi recently, don't worry about the kombu.

BEAUTIFUL, SIMPLE, BEAUTIFULLY SIMPLE SASHIMI

刺身の盛り合わせの簡単な作り方 SASHIMI NO MORIAWASE NO KANTAN NA TSUKURIKATA

SERVES 2–4

50 g (2 oz) daikon, peeled,
    or radishes
iced water
60–70 g (2–3 oz) each sashimi-grade
    salmon, tuna and sea bream,
    or similar
3 leaves of fresh shiso,
    nasturtium, or similar firm,
    large, peppery leaves
2 tbsp good-quality soy sauce
½–1 tbsp prepared wasabi,
    or more to taste

While sushi is sometimes served in izakaya, it's far more common to find sashimi, typically ordered as a set called *moriawase* rather than à la carte. Sushi is more of a production than sashimi, mainly due to the preparation of the rice and the process of shaping each individual piece. Sashimi offers a similar eating experience, showcasing the pure flavours and textures of top-quality raw seafood, but it's much simpler to prepare. And that's good news if you're trying to recreate an izakaya experience at home.

I am awestruck when I watch experienced sushi chefs work, amazed by everything from how they cook and season their rice to how they prepare their toppings to how their hands move when they shape each piece of nigiri. It's mesmerising, and I think something best left to the professionals. Sashimi, on the other hand, is more my tempo – in its simplest, purest form, it's just neatly sliced fish. But, I would still recommend outsourcing most of the work to an actual fishmonger.

By far the easiest way to make sashimi at home is to cut it from blocks sold frozen at Japanese supermarkets or specialist online fish suppliers. Pre-cut and portioned into neat rectangles called *saku*, all they require you to do is thaw them out and slice them. Frozen sashimi blocks are good quality and very safe to eat, but they are not cheap.

The next-best option for hygienic, tasty, user-friendly sashimi is your trusted local fishmonger. Even if they don't specialise in sashimi-grade fish, if you tell them what you need they'll be able to get good-quality stuff, and prepare it to your specifications. The recipe provided here uses tuna, salmon and sea bream, which all have different preparations, but in the case of salmon and bream, it's as simple as asking for just the loin of the fish, skinned and pin-boned. Tuna is a bit more complicated because you'll need a block cut from the eye of the loin, but even this should not be outside a typical fishmonger's repertoire.

I haven't chosen these three fish arbitrarily, by the way. They present a nice variety of textures, flavours and colours; they're easy to source and prepare; and they're crowd-pleasers. But feel free to choose whatever fish you like; I would recommend sticking with one red, one white and one pink (or orange), but that's mainly because it looks nice.

(Cont. overleaf)

By the way, if you're really not sure about the quality and freshness of your fishmonger's offerings, ask to have a very close look at them before you buy. The flesh should be vibrant in colour (pearly and bright, if it's white fish) and have an aroma that's mild, fresh and oceanic, not strong and fishy. It's also best practice to freeze fresh fish for 24 hours before you eat it, as this kills most parasites and microbes that it may be harbouring.

Really, sourcing fish is the hard part – and it ain't that hard. Once you've got that squared away, making a lovely sashimi platter is quite achievable.

METHOD

Slice the daikon or radishes very, very thinly – use a mandoline if you have one, and if you don't, use a very sharp knife and take your time. Cut down the length of the daikon to get slices. Stack the slices of daikon up and cut them again into very thin shreds. Transfer these to a bowl of cold water with a few ice cubes and leave to soak while you prepare the fish (if you don't have ice, just put the bowl in the fridge for about 20 minutes).

Slice the fish with a very sharp knife, across the grain and with one long stroke, not with a back-and-forth sawing motion. If the fish itself is quite thin, cut at an angle to give the slices some extra height. Each piece should be no more than about 6 mm (¼ in) thick; you should get 5–6 slices out of each block. To serve, drain the daikon very well, then place it in a pile on a small plate. Rest two shiso or nasturtium leaves on the bed of daikon, then lay the sashimi slices out on top of the leaves. Place the third leaf on top of the two types of fish, and lay the third type of sashimi on top, in the centre. Serve with the soy sauce and the wasabi on the side.

MEAL FOR TWO WITH	PAIR WITH
Squid and Spring Onions with Citrus Miso (page 44), plain rice and miso soup.	Sake – the nicest, most refined sake you have! Or green tea.

TIP

You can't cut tuna sashimi from tuna steaks; the slices will fall apart; you need to get a solid block of tuna for this.

WASABI-MARINATED OCTOPUS WITH OKRA

たこわさとオクラのグリル　**TAKOWASA TO OKURA NO GURIRU**

One of the very first izakaya meals I had in Japan was somewhere in Tokyo, fresh off the boat en route to my tour of duty as an English teacher in Kyushu. My Japanese language ability has never really been more than rudimentary, but at that point I couldn't even read most menus. So I ordered basically just the few things I *could* read – one of which was *tako-wasa*, written in the simpler *hiragana* orthography, as opposed to *kanji*, which is highly complex. I had no idea what tako-wasa was, but I correctly guessed it contained octopus (*tako*) and wasabi. It turned out there wasn't much more to it than that: just raw octopus, chopped up, then marinated in a generous amount of piquant wasabi and other simple seasonings. It's pretty hard to source octopus that's fit to serve raw in the UK, so in this recipe, the octopus is cooked. Raw octopus also has a delightfully slippery-slimy texture, so to replicate that, I include a bit of okra. But if you can get sashimi-quality raw octopus, by all means have a go with that. Also, if you can't get octopus at all, this would be quite good with squid or cuttlefish instead.

METHOD

If your octopus is raw, cook it. Bring a large pan of water to a high simmer, then lower in the octopus and cook for 45 minutes–1 hour until tender but not soft (it should still be slightly chewy). Drain well, then transfer to a roasting tin and leave to air-dry for 10 minutes or so. Mince two of the okra pods and cut the other two into slices about 5 mm (¼ in) thick. Combine the wasabi, mirin, sake, dashi powder, sugar, salt, minced okra and chilli, if using, stirring well to dissolve the sugar. Place the octopus under a very hot grill (broiler) and cook for a few minutes on each side until lightly charred. Dice the octopus into bite-size chunks and mix with the sauce along with the sliced okra. Enjoy straight away or leave in the fridge to marinate for a few hours, up to two days. Serve at room temperature or cold, garnished with the lemon wedge and chopped chives.

SERVES 2

2 large or 4 small octopus tentacles, raw or cooked (this is about 300 g (10½ oz) raw or 150–200 g (5–7 oz) cooked)
4 okra pods
1 tbsp prepared wasabi
1 tbsp mirin
1 tbsp sake
¼ tsp dashi powder (kombu rather than katsuo, if possible) or MSG
½ tsp sugar
2–3 pinches of salt
½ dried red chilli, finely snipped with scissors, or 1 pinch of red chilli (hot pepper) flakes (optional)
¼ lemon
1 small handful of chives, chopped

MEAL FOR TWO WITH	PAIR WITH
Karaage 6.0 (page 104) and Baked Potatoes with Butter and Salmon Roe (page 86).	Green tea, whisky, dry sherry or rough, savoury sake.

SQUID AND SPRING ONIONS WITH CITRUS MISO

イカとネギの柚子味噌炒め　IKA TO NEGI NO YUZUMISO ITAME

While some izakaya dishes are big, fat party animals that love being the centre of attention, others, like this one, are more like the chill, slyly funny guy who hangs out in the kitchen and gradually becomes your new favourite person over the course of the evening. The flavours here are alternately meaty, fishy, fresh, earthy, fruity, sweet, sour, subtle and strong, but never aggressive or overbearing. It's quietly complex, fun and lively, yet satisfyingly deep. It's everything I've always wanted in a BFF, but in a squid dish.

METHOD

Slice the spring onions at an angle into long chunks about 1 cm (½ in) thick. Whisk together the miso, sugar, mirin, lime zest and citrus juice until the sugar has dissolved and no lumps of miso remain. Pat the squid tubes dry with paper towels, then cut them in half lengthways to make fillets. Score them with a sharp knife, about every 2–3 mm (⅛ in), in a diamond pattern, then cut into bite-size rectangles. Leave the tentacles whole (if you have them). Heat the oil in a wok or frying pan (skillet) over a very high heat until it is smoking, then add the squid and stir-fry rapidly for about 3–4 minutes until cooked through and lightly charred. Remove the squid and return the pan to the heat, then add the spring onions and stir-fry for a minute, then add the sauce, reduce the heat to low, and stir in the cooked squid. Remove from the heat, toss everything well and serve.

SERVES 2

½ bunch (50–60 g/2 oz) spring
　onions (scallions)
60 g (2 oz) white miso
15 g (½ oz) sugar
2 tbsp mirin
very finely grated zest of 1 lime
1 tbsp yuzu juice, or a mixture
　of lime and grapefruit juice
about 400 g (14 oz) squid, cleaned
1 tsp oil

MEAL FOR TWO WITH
Rice Soup (page 154).

PAIR WITH
Chilled sake, fruity white wine
or green tea.

TIP
If you are lucky enough to get fresh yuzu or frozen yuzu peel, replace the lime zest with that.

LIGHTLY PICKLED CUCUMBERS WITH GARLIC AND SESAME OIL

やみつきぎゅうりのごま油にんにく和え

YAMITSUKI KYŪRI NO GOMAYU NINNIKU AE

Like the cabbage recipe on page 33, this simple but effective cucumber pickle recipe is addictive. And if you're going to be addicted to something, cucumbers are probably among the most benign things you can go for. This can be a side dish all on its own, or you can just serve a few chunks of the pickled cucumbers alongside a larger meal.

SERVES 2–4

1 cucumber, ends removed
2 garlic cloves, grated
1 tbsp sesame oil
4 tbsp vinegar
2 tbsp soy sauce
1 tbsp sugar
¼ tsp MSG
1 pinch of white pepper
2 tsp sesame seeds
a pinch of shichimi or chilli (hot pepper) flakes (optional)

METHOD

Cut the cucumber into thirds, then each third into quarters, so you have 12 triangular prism-shaped cucumber batons. Combine these with all the other ingredients except the shichimi or chilli, if using, in a plastic bag, seal it and shake it up. Leave to marinate for at least 4 hours or up to a day, shaking the bag again whenever you think of it. Serve in a dish with the marinade poured over the top, and garnish with the shichimi or chilli, if you like.

MEAL FOR TWO WITH

Spicy Sesame Ramen Salad (page 159).

PAIR WITH

Pale ale, shōchū or oolong tea.

STIR-FRIED BEANSPROUTS WITH DRIED CHILLI

もやしの赤唐辛子炒め

MOYASHI NO AKATŌGARASHI ITAME

Beansprouts are essentially crunchy water: all texture, no flavour. But I don't say that as a bad thing; quite the contrary, sometimes all you *want* is texture, and beansprouts are pretty much unrivalled in their ability to deliver that. This recipe sees their refreshing crunch paired with the spicy kick of dried chillies and a light glaze of sesame oil. It is a side dish par excellence for fatty meats or oily fish.

SERVES 2–4

1 dried red chilli, finely snipped with scissors,
    or ¼ tsp chilli (hot pepper) flakes
1 tbsp sesame oil
300–350 g (10½–12 oz) beansprouts
2 tsp soy sauce
½ tsp MSG or chicken stock powder
½ tsp sugar
1 garlic clove, minced or finely grated

METHOD

Heat the chilli and sesame oil together in a wok or frying pan (skillet) over a medium–high heat. When the chilli begins to sizzle, add the beansprouts and sprinkle over the seasonings. Increase the heat to high, add the garlic and quickly stir-fry for 4–5 minutes until the beansprouts have softened very slightly but still retain their crunch. This can be served hot or cold.

MEAL FOR TWO WITH

Crispy Noodle Modanyaki (page 150)
or any other noodle dish

PAIR WITH

Amber ale, rich sake or barley tea.

SAKE-STEAMED CLAMS

あさりの酒蒸し　ASARI NO SAKAMUSHI

Just like sashimi (page 39), clams steamed in sake boast an enormous deliciousness-to-effort ratio; they are so simple they almost don't require a recipe, and the resulting broth of clam juice and sake is like an umami supernova. But also like sashimi, they rely on good-quality fresh ingredients; in this case, you need to make sure you get good, fresh clams that are free of grit. The only way to really guarantee this is to buy them from a trusted fishmonger. There are only three places where I trust the clams in London. Which is not to say there aren't more sources of good clams, it's just that now that I've found three, why would I take a risk on anywhere else? So find yourself a reliable clam guy and hold onto him forever.

Nira, or garlic chives, are an excellent alternative to leeks in this recipe, if you can get them. They are sold at any Asian supermarket, usually under their Chinese name, *kow choi*.

METHOD

Wash the clams under running water; if you can see or feel any dirt or grit on them, scrub it off. Check that all the clams' shells are closed and intact; discard any that are broken or that are open and don't close when you tap them. Place the sake, leeks or nira and garlic in a frying pan (skillet) and bring to the boil, then tip in the clams and place a lid on the pan. Steam for about 4 minutes until all the clams have opened up. Remove the lid then add the parsley and toss it through, cooking for another minute or so. Remove from the heat and discard any clams that have not opened. Serve piping hot, and make sure you have some rice or bread on hand to soak up the juice.

SERVES 2

400–500 g (14 oz–1 lb 2 oz) clams
100 ml (3½ fl oz/scant ½ cup) sake
½ leek, cut in half and thinly sliced at an angle, or 2 stalks of *nira* (garlic chives), cut into 2 cm (¾ in) chunks
1 garlic clove, minced or finely grated
a few sprigs of flat-leaf parsley, finely chopped

MEAL FOR TWO WITH
'Japaniçoise' Salad (page 65) and crusty bread.

PAIR WITH
Sake, white wine, highballs or iced oolong tea.

TOMATOES MARINATED IN GINGER TSUYU

トマトの生姜つゆ漬け　TOMATO NO SHŌGA TSUYU ZUKE

I was in a taiko drumming group in Japan – an extremely warm and friendly bunch of people who were responsible for many of the best food experiences I had there, such as my first offal hotpot, a tonkotsu ramen crawl around Fukuoka, a farmhouse feast in rural Kumamoto, and all manner of fine fresh produce they procured from friends and relatives in the countryside. In July, we performed in the city's biggest festival, Kokura Gion, which was fun but exhausting. At some point we took a break, and somebody handed me a tomato they said was grown in a friend's garden. I took a bite and perked up immediately; it was so sweet, so vibrant, with tender skin and just the right amount of acidity. We all sat on the asphalt, eating tomatoes and marvelling at how good they were until it was time to get up and drum some more.

That's what I think of when I think of this dish: a little something zingy to give you a bit of pep. The sauce here enhances the tomatoes' natural umami and sweetness, while the ginger makes them even more vibrant. Use the best tomatoes you can get for this, and serve them straight out of the fridge.

METHOD

Cut a cross through the skin at the bottom of each tomato and bring a saucepan of water to the boil. Blanch the tomatoes for 1 minute, then remove and transfer to a bowl of ice water. Once chilled, drain the tomatoes and peel off their skins. Remove their stems and cores with a paring knife, and cut the tomatoes into quarters. Transfer the tomatoes to a container just big enough to fit them in a single layer.

Finely chop the katsuobushi (if using) and combine with the tsuyu and ginger in a saucepan. Bring to the boil over a medium heat, then remove from the heat and pour over the tomatoes. Leave to marinate in the fridge overnight. Serve the tomatoes chilled, in some of their sauce, topped with a few bits of katsuobushi and ginger. Any leftover tsuyu can be re-used, and will be even tastier, having picked up the flavour of the ginger and tomatoes.

SERVES 2–4

250–300 g (9–10½ oz) tomatoes – any kind will do, but I like ones that are small-ish in size, about 4–5 cm (1½–2 in) in diameter

100 ml (3½ fl oz/scant ½ cup) tsuyu, store-bought or homemade (page 220), plus 1 tbsp of rehydrated katsuobushi from making it (optional)

1 cm (½ in) piece of ginger root, peeled and very finely chopped

MEAL FOR TWO WITH
Ham and Cheese Mille-Feuille Katsu (page 106) and plain rice.

PAIR WITH
Sake, dry sherry or green tea.

CUCUMBER WITH PICKLED PLUMS, SHISO AND KATSUOBUSHI

きゅうりの梅しそ和え
KYŪRI NO UME-SHISO AE

One of my all-time favourite flavour combinations is *umeshiso*: bracingly sour, salty pickled plums (*umeboshi*) mixed with fragrant shiso, a peppery Japanese herb. The problem is, both of these ingredients are annoyingly hard to find here in the UK, but I'm including this recipe anyway to encourage you to seek them out, because the combination really is spectacular. Umeshiso is used to flavour all kinds of dishes (try it with cheese on toast!), but I think my first experience with it was at our regular yakitori joint, where the master would sometimes whip up this simple snack of cucumbers dressed with umeshiso mixed with a little bit of katsuobushi. It is superb with beer or shōchū.

SERVES 2
2 umeboshi, stones removed, finely chopped, or 1 tbsp umeboshi purée
1 tsp sugar
½ tsp soy sauce
½ cucumber, cut into batons or chunky slices
3 leaves of shiso, roughly torn
1 small handful of katsuobushi (you can use the spent/rehydrated katsuobushi from making dashi or tsuyu for this, page 220)

METHOD

In a mixing bowl, stir together the umeboshi, sugar and soy sauce until the sugar has dissolved. Toss through the cucumber, shiso and katsuobushi. Serve quickly after preparing because the salt will start to draw water out of the cucumber and dilute the seasoning.

MEAL FOR TWO WITH
Yakitori (page 139) and plain rice.

PAIR WITH
Lager, umeshu soda or oolong.

CHILLED TOFU WITH EGG YOLK, CHILLI OIL AND SPRING ONION

冷奴の卵黄とラ一油添え
HIYAYAKKO NO RANŌ TO RĀYU SOE

Hiyayakko – a simple assemblage of chilled silken tofu with soy sauce, spring onions, katsuobushi and ginger – is one of my all-time favourite things to eat on a hot day. Variations on this dish abound, and at izakaya it's common to find hiyayakko with a spicy twist, laced with a generous amount of chilli oil – any kind will do, but I like the kinds with bits you can eat in it. For me, this is what izakaya cooking is all about: food that's huge on flavour but also simple and balanced.

SERVES 2
1 tbsp chilli oil
1 tbsp soy sauce
½ tbsp mirin
½ tsp vinegar
1 egg yolk
350 g (12 oz/1 block) firm silken tofu
1 spring onion (scallion), finely sliced

METHOD

Combine the chilli oil, soy sauce, mirin and vinegar in a very small dish or container, then carefully lower the yolk into the liquid. Leave it to sit in the fridge for about 30 minutes, which will cure the yolk slightly and make it richer. Remove the tofu from the package and drain it well, blotting it dry with paper towels. Transfer to a plate and scoop a little egg yolk-shaped hollow out of the centre. Spoon the yolk into the hollow, then pour the liquid all over the tofu. Top with the spring onion.

MEAL FOR TWO WITH
Sea Bream Nanban-zuke (page 108) and plain rice.

PAIR WITH
German-style wheat beer or barley tea.

BRAISED DAIKON
WITH MISO SAUCE

風呂吹き大根　*FUROFUKI DAIKON*

SERVES 2

about 300 g (10½ oz/roughly ¼
    large) daikon, peeled and cut into
    four 2.5 cm (1 in) thick rounds
500 ml (17 fl oz/2 cups) water
    (ideally from washing rice)
500 ml (17 fl oz/2 cups) fresh water
10 cm (4 in) square piece of kombu
1 tbsp soy sauce
¼ tsp salt
2 tbsp white miso
1 tbsp mirin
½ tbsp sugar
1 tsp sake
½ tbsp yuzu juice
a few shreds of yuzu or
    lemon peel (optional)

This absolute classic of izakaya cuisine has a name that roughly translates as 'piping hot daikon', but it can also be read as 'steaming bath daikon'. I love the idea of a daikon chilling out in a hot bath, with Enya playing softly in the background and a glass of red wine off to the side. And this dish is every bit as soothing and lovely as its name suggests: long-braised daikon in subtle dashi, topped with a moreish miso sauce. Traditionally, this is made with the starchy water which is usually discarded when washing rice; it is said to make the daikon less bitter, which I don't think is true, but even so, it is a lovely way to reclaim something that would otherwise be wasted.

METHOD

Run a knife along the hard edges at the circumferences of each slice of daikon so they are more rounded; this technique is called *mentori*. It makes them less likely to break and also makes them look nice, like little cushions. Combine the first 500 ml (17 fl oz/ 2 cups) of water and the daikon in a saucepan and bring to a high simmer. Cook with a lid on the pan for about 45 minutes until the daikon is tender. Drain and discard the liquid. Return the cooked daikon to the pan with the fresh water, kombu, soy sauce and salt, and once again bring to a high simmer. Remove the kombu and set aside. Cook the daikon for another 30 minutes until it is very soft (you should be able to slip a butter knife into it with no resistance).

Meanwhile, make the sauce by combining the miso, mirin, sugar, sake and yuzu juice, stirring to dissolve the miso and sugar. To serve, lay the kombu square out on the bottom of a shallow dish. Cut each daikon round into four bite-size quarters, but keep each round together. Place them on the kombu, then pour over some of the braising liquid. Top each piece with a spoonful of the miso sauce and garnish with the citrus peel.

MEAL FOR TWO WITH
Like edamame, this is sort of a prelude to a meal rather than a course in and of itself.

PAIR WITH
Table sake or green tea.

AVOCADO SASHIMI WITH GUACAMOLE GARNISHES

ワカモレ味のアボカド刺身

WAKAMORE AJI NO ABOKADO SASHIMI

This sliced avocado dish is a perennial favourite at izakaya and in home kitchens in Japan, thanks to its foolproof, crowd-pleasing nature. Often it's served with accoutrements typical to actual sashimi – such as ponzu, wasabi and soy sauce – but I've seen it seasoned with punchier things, too, like garlic, katsuobushi and chilli oil. This version uses ingredients found in guacamole: tomato, garlic, onion, lime, chilli and coriander. If you think this sounds like an obnoxious fusion recipe from 20 years ago, you are not wrong, but consider this: it's really tasty! And in an izakaya, that's kind of all that matters. This is good with beer or sake but I would highly encourage you to have this with shōchū or mezcal instead.

METHOD

Slice the red onion as thinly as you can and place in a small dish. Cover with cold water and add an ice cube, which will make it extra crispy and remove some of the harsh raw onion flavour. Scorch the tomato all over by holding it with tongs over the flame on your hob, or by setting it under a very, very hot grill, turning frequently until its skin is completely charred. Remove the tomato skin, core and finely dice the flesh, then combine the chopped tomato and any of its juice with the garlic, ponzu, sesame oil and salt. Cut the avocado open and remove the stone, scoop out the flesh from each half in one piece with a spoon, then cut each side into 6–8 slices. Arrange the slices on a plate, then spoon over the tomato ponzu mixture, drain the onions and place on top with the jalapeño and coriander leaves.

SERVES 2

⅛ red onion
1 tomato
½ garlic clove, minced or finely grated
2 tbsp ponzu, store-bought or homemade (page 222)
½ tsp sesame oil
1 pinch of salt
1 avocado
¼ jalapeño, very thinly sliced
10–12 coriander (cilantro) leaves, picked

MEAL FOR TWO WITH
Japanese Fish and Chips (page 103) or Okinawan Taco Rice, Bibimbap-style (page 132).

PAIR WITH
Tequila, mezcal, shōchū or amber lager.

MISO-MARINATED TOFU 'CHEESE'

豆腐の味噌漬け **TŌFU NO MISOZUKE**

SERVES 4

250–300 g (9–10½ oz/1 block)
  cotton tofu
3 tbsp miso (I prefer dark miso
  but any kind will do)
1 tbsp mirin
good-quality olive oil, to taste
a few flakes of sea salt

I often describe miso to the uninitiated as a bit like cheese. It is, of course, mostly NOT like cheese, but some of its flavours can be quite cheesy – simultaneously fruity, earthy, nutty, salty, tangy, sweet, fresh and rich. Tofu is also something often compared to cheese, but tofu is unlike cheese in the opposite way: it doesn't have any strong, cheesy flavours, just a similar process of making it, and a vaguely cheese-like texture. Which brings us quite neatly to *tofu no misozuke*: tofu marinated in miso. This traditional Japanese preparation combines the cheesy texture of tofu with the cheesy flavour of miso, making something remarkably cheesy indeed, an ideal Japanese snack if wine is your tipple of choice.

METHOD

In order for the tofu to properly absorb the marinade, it has to be well drained. You can either do this in the fridge overnight or quite quickly in the microwave. It all depends on how much time you have. Either way, place your tofu into a dish with a flat bottom and place another small dish on top of it to weigh it down. To drain it in the fridge, simply leave it there for 12–24 hours, then discard the liquid and pat it dry with paper towels. To drain it in the microwave, zap it for 30 seconds, then drain off any liquid it releases, turn the tofu over and repeat. Leave to sit with the plate on top for an additional 15–20 minutes to cool down and press out additional water. Drain and pat dry with paper towels and ensure the tofu is at room temperature or cooler before proceeding with this recipe.

Stir together the miso and mirin to make a thick paste. Spread this paste all over the tofu, then wrap it in two sheets of food-safe paper towels or muslin. Wrap the cloth-wrapped tofu in cling film (plastic wrap) and place in a container with a lid in the fridge. Leave to marinate for 2 weeks, then remove the paper towels and scrape off the excess miso paste. Slice and serve drizzled with a little olive oil and scattered with sea salt.

MEAL FOR TWO WITH

This is best served as
a pre-meal appetiser.

PAIR WITH

Light red wine, dry sake,
sour beer or kombucha.

CREAM CHEESE WITH JAPANESE PICKLES

クリームチーズ漬物添え KURĪMU CHĪZU TSUKEMONO SOE

It's sometimes surprising that dairy wasn't a part of Japanese gastronomy until the late 19th century, considering how delicious cheese is with so many Japanese flavours. A perennial izakaya favourite is a simple blend of cream cheese with Japanese pickles, most commonly *Nara-zuke*: various fruits and vegetables preserved in sweet sake lees. Nara-zuke is very difficult to find outside Japan, but all sorts of Japanese pickles work well in this combo; cream cheese is pure, mellow dairy richness, while *tsukemono* are tangy and assertive in flavour and texture, so the two complement each other perfectly. You can try this with *fukujin-zuke*, the crunchy sweet-and-sour mixed vegetable pickle most commonly served with curry; umeboshi, intensely sour pickled plums; or *iburigakko*, smoked and pickled daikon as leathery and complex as an Islay whisky. Use whatever you like – I don't think you can go wrong here. Even *gari*, pickled ginger for sushi, is good!

METHOD

Mix the cheese and pickles together. Enjoy on its own or on crackers.

SERVES 2

100 g (3½ oz) cream cheese
30–40 g (1–1½ oz) Japanese pickles, coarsely chopped

TIP

The quantities here are just a guide; you can adjust this however you like, depending on how strong your pickles are. (For example, if you are using umeboshi, which are extremely strong, you probably won't need more than 10 g (½ oz) for 100 g (3½ oz) of cheese.)

MEAL FOR TWO WITH	**PAIR WITH**
This is more of a snack rather than a side dish. Serve it with drinks before the meal.	This was made for sake or wine but it would also be damn good with a martini.

POTATO SALAD WITH RAMEN EGGS

味付け卵のポテトサラダ　AJITSUKE TAMAGO NO POTETO SARADA

SERVES 4

250 g (9 oz) potatoes – use a fluffy,
    floury variety like Maris Piper
    or King Edward
5 cm (2 in) chunk of cucumber
½ small carrot
salt, as needed
2 cornichons
about 30 g (1 oz) ham (I like a very
    smoky ham for this)
60 g (2 oz) mayo, ideally Japanese
¼ tsp dashi powder or MSG
¼ tsp mustard (any kind)
1 pinch each of salt and pepper,
    or more to taste
1 pinch of garlic powder (optional)
4 Ramen Eggs (page 223)
1 small handful of chives,
    finely chopped

Most potato salads wouldn't make particularly good drinking food. But most potato salads aren't Japanese potato salad. Japanese potato salad is the best in the world and I will fight anyone who says otherwise. The potatoes are partially mashed with a generous amount of mayo, so it has a gorgeously airy, creamy texture – like a cold potato cloud – and it's studded with crunchy-salty bits like sliced carrots and cucumber as well as ham, so every mouthful is delightfully different. Often, Japanese potato salad also contains eggs and occasionally these are the always-a-good-idea *ajitsuke tamago*, more commonly known in English as ramen eggs. They add a savoury depth and richness for some seriously superlative potato salad.

METHOD

Wash the potatoes and cut them into big chunks, about 3 cm (¼ in), thick, similar to how you would prepare them for roasting, but with the skins on. Place in a saucepan and cover with water, then bring to the boil and cook until fork-tender, about 10–12 minutes. Drain well and leave to dry out and cool completely, then remove their skins.

Meanwhile, cut the cucumber and carrot in half lengthways, then slice them very thinly (no more than 2 mm (⅛ in) thick) into little half rounds. Sprinkle them with a generous amount of salt, massage it into the vegetables, then leave them for 30 minutes to tenderise. Rinse them well under cold running water to remove the salt, and squeeze out any excess liquid. Dice the cornichons and cut the ham into thin strips.

Stir together the mayo, dashi powder or MSG, mustard, salt, pepper and garlic powder, if using. With a fork or sturdy whisk, mix the mayo mixture into the cooked and cooled potatoes somewhat violently – you want to break up the potatoes and half-mash them to give the salad a fluffy, creamy texture. Mix in the cucumbers, carrots, cornichons and ham, then taste and adjust the seasoning to your liking. Break or chop the ramen eggs up into coarse chunks and scatter them over the salad. Top with chopped chives and serve.

MEAL FOR TWO WITH	PAIR WITH
Something meaty like Roast Pork (page 84) or Karaage 6.0 (page 104) would be ideal.	German or Czech lager or cold barley tea.

RAW TUNA WITH GRATED RADISH AND PONZU

鮪の大根おろしポン酢和え

MAGURO NO DAIKON OROSHI PONZU AE

I think tuna is best served raw or only seared so you can fully enjoy its supple texture and rich flavour. This preparation is not dissimilar to the globally popular Hawaiian poke, with raw tuna simply dressed with grated radish and sweetened ponzu, providing a light acidity to balance the strong flavour of the fish.

SERVES 2

3 tbsp ponzu, store-bought or homemade (page 222)
1 tsp sugar
200 g (7 oz) raw, fresh tuna loin or steak
50 g (2 oz) daikon, peeled, or radishes
1 spring onion (scallion), finely sliced

METHOD

Stir together the ponzu and the sugar until the sugar has dissolved. Cut the tuna into chunks no larger than 2 cm (¾ in) wide. Finely grate the daikon or radish, then squeeze it to remove any excess liquid. Pile the tuna into a bowl with the grated radish, then pour over the sweetened ponzu, stir it up a bit and garnish with the spring onions.

MEAL FOR TWO WITH

Grilled Broccoli with White Miso and Sesame Sauce (page 66), plain rice and miso soup.

PAIR WITH

Sake or green tea.

'JAPANIÇOISE' SALAD

サラダジャパニーソワーズ

SARADA JAPANĪSOWĀZU

You won't find this salad on any izakaya menu that I know of, but I just can't resist a good pun. Really, this is just the key components of a classic Niçoise salad with a Japanese dressing, which makes it not very different from a typical wafū (Japanese-style) salad anyway. I've left out the usual olives because they would be quite unusual to find on an izakaya menu, but anyway I don't think this salad needs them – there's enough salt and acidity from the dressing.

SERVES 2 AS A MAIN DISH, 4 AS A SIDE

250 g (9 oz) baby potatoes
2 tsp dashi powder
4 tbsp soy sauce
100 g (3½ oz) fine green beans, trimmed and cut into chunks about 5 cm (2 in) long
2 Ramen Eggs (page 223)
1 little gem lettuce, roughly chopped
150 g (5 oz) cherry tomatoes, halved
200 g (7 oz) tin of tuna, drained
90 ml (3 fl oz/⅓ cup) Wafu Dressing (page 222)

METHOD

Place the potatoes in a saucepan, cover with water and add the dashi powder and soy sauce. Bring to the boil and cook until just tender, about 8 minutes, then add the beans (top up the water if necessary) and cook for another 2–3 minutes until the potatoes are completely cooked through. Drain the beans and potatoes, then chill in the fridge. Cut the marinated eggs in half. Gently crush the potatoes with your hands so their skins split, then toss them with the beans, lettuce, tomatoes, tuna and dressing. Serve with the eggs on top.

MEAL FOR TWO WITH

Miso-marinated Tofu Cheese (page 59) and rice or bread.

PAIR WITH

Crisp rosé wine or fancy sparkling mineral water, perhaps infused with cucumber (ooh la la).

GRILLED BROCCOLI WITH WHITE MISO AND SESAME SAUCE

ブロッコリーの ごま味噌和え
BUROKKORĪ NO GOMAMISO-AE

In Japan, prime seasonal vegetables may be fetishised just as much as meat or fish and prepared with just as much care and attention. Famously rare and expensive *matsutake* mushrooms, for example, are often simply but carefully grilled and served with sea salt and a tiny bit of *sudachi* citrus, to showcase and enhance their beautiful evergreen aroma. This recipe uses broccoli, which admittedly is a lot more boring than *matsutake* mushrooms, but the point stands: as long as you cook and season them nicely, vegetables will be just as delicious as anything else on the table. This sauce is versatile enough to work with pretty much any vegetable, so you can change it up with the seasons – asparagus is particularly good.

SERVES 2

1 tbsp white miso
1 tbsp sesame seeds, crushed or milled
    to the consistency of coarse sand
1 tbsp mirin
2 tsp yuzu or lemon juice
2 tsp sesame oil
1 tsp sugar
200 g (7 oz) broccoli (long-stem or florets)

METHOD

Preheat the grill (broiler) to very high. Stir together all of the seasonings until the sugar dissolves and no lumps of miso remain. Bring a saucepan of water to the boil and blanch the broccoli for about 2 minutes until tender but still slightly crunchy in the middle, then drain very well and transfer to a baking tray. Grill (broil) the broccoli for 4–5 minutes, turning a few times until lightly charred. Transfer to a plate and serve with the sauce drizzled on top, or on the side as a dip.

MEAL FOR TWO WITH
Grilled Broccoli with White Miso and Sesame Sauce (page 66), plain rice and miso soup.

PAIR WITH
Sake or green tea.

SAUTÉED PEA SHOOTS WITH CRUSHED SESAME

豆苗のごま和え
TŌMYŌ NO GOMA-AE

In the UK we usually eat pea shoots raw, which is nice, but they're also a fantastic vegetable to cook with. They hold their crunch and their colour well, and cooking them seems to enhance their naturally sweet-savoury pea flavour. In Japan they are used in stir-fries or soups, and they're an ideal choice for *goma-ae*, the classic preparation of lightly seasoned vegetables with a generous amount of crushed sesame seeds.

SERVES 2

1 tbsp sesame oil
120–150 g (4–5 oz) pea shoots
1 tbsp sake
1 tbsp soy sauce
1 tsp sugar
¼ tsp dashi powder or MSG
2 tbsp sesame seeds, crushed or milled
    to the consistency of coarse sand
salt, to taste

METHOD

Heat the sesame oil in a frying pan (skillet) or wok over a medium heat, then add the pea shoots and all of the seasonings and increase the heat to high. Stir-fry until the liquid has evaporated and the pea shoots are wilted but still bright green, about 2 minutes. Remove from the heat, stir in the sesame seeds, taste, and adjust seasoning with salt as necessary.

MEAL FOR TWO WITH
Steamed Egg Tofu with Mapo Sauce (page 89) and plain rice.

PAIR WITH
Jasmine tea or wheat beer.

These dishes are meatier, fattier, cheesier and generally more weighty than those in the previous chapter. If Japanese food could be described as 'meat and two veg' – and sometimes it can – then this would be the meat, often literally. You'll want to pair these with something lighter (even if it's just pickles or salad from a bag) and you'll also probably want rice or some other carb to go with them and round out the meal.

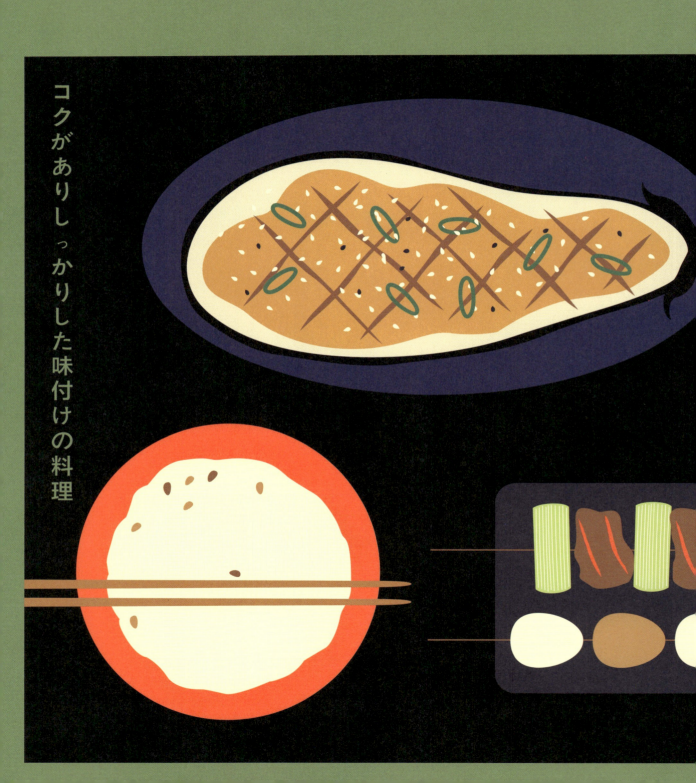

コクがありしっかりした味付けの料理

BOLD & BURLY

CHEESE CRACKERS WITH SESAME AND NORI

和風チーズせんべい　WAFŪ CHĪZU SENBEI

MAKES 10–12 CRACKERS

---

75 g (2½ oz) Edam, Gouda or similar mild cheese, grated
30 g (1 oz) Parmesan, grated
¼ sheet of nori, finely chopped or snipped with scissors into tiny flakes, or 1 tbsp aonori flakes
1 tbsp white or black sesame seeds

In Britain, crisps made of grated cheese are mainly the domain of fancy restaurants, who use them as a garnish or a flavoursome base for amuse-bouches and canapés. But in Japan they're usually just a quick drinking snack that anybody with a microwave can make. They're typically made from quite mild cheese (the norm in Japan) but I've included a bit of Parmesan for extra flavour here, because I think it has a special affinity with beer and sake.

METHOD

Combine the cheeses, nori and sesame seeds.

To cook in a microwave, line a flat, microwave-safe plate with baking parchment, then place little circles of the cheese mixture on the paper – you'll only be able to fit three or four at a time, so you'll have to do this in batches. Microwave for 90 seconds – the cheese should melt, fuse together and brown lightly. If it doesn't, keep zapping it in 20-second intervals until completely melted and brown along the edges. Leave the crackers to set slightly before removing from the paper. Cool completely on paper towels or a wire rack before eating.

To cook in the oven, heat the oven to 200°C (400°F/gas mark 7). Line one or two roasting tins with baking parchment, then place little circles of the cheese mixture on the paper. Bake for 10 minutes until the cheese melts and browns lightly. Leave the crackers to set for a few minutes before removing from the paper. Cool completely on paper towels or a wire rack before eating.

To cook in a pan, place a non-stick, flat-bottomed frying pan (skillet) over a medium–high heat, then place little circles of the cheese mixture directly into the pan – you'll only be able to fit three or four at a time, so you'll have to do this in batches. Cook for a few minutes until the cheese melts, fuses together and browns. Remove from the heat and leave for a few minutes to allow the cheese to cool and set, then remove from the pan with a spatula and cool completely on paper towels or a wire rack before eating. Eat ASAP as they lose their crunch after a day.

MEAL FOR TWO WITH	PAIR WITH
Drinks! (It's really a snack, rather than a dish.)	The kind of red wine you can serve chilled, or sake or a proper IPA.

STIR-FRIED CABBAGE AND BACON IN CURRY BUTTER SAUCE

キャベツとベーコンのカレーバター炒め KYABETSU TO BĒKON NO KARĒ BATĀ ITAME

SERVES 2

1 tbsp oil
4 slices of streaky bacon,
    cut into 2.5 cm (1 in) chunks
½ onion, thinly sliced
½ sweetheart (hispi) cabbage, cored
    and coarsely chopped
1 heaped tbsp mild curry powder
30 g (1 oz) butter
90 ml (3 fl oz/⅔ cup) chicken stock
    (from a cube is fine)
a splash of water
salt, to taste

Curry is so popular in Japan that the flavour frequently works its way into other dishes. It lends a warming, aromatic character to fried chicken, mashed potato croquettes or simple stir-fries like this one, which also features the always-delicious combination of cabbage, bacon and butter.

METHOD

Heat the oil in a large frying pan (skillet) or wok over a medium–high heat, then add the bacon and onions. Fry for about 5 minutes until lightly browned. Add the cabbage, curry powder and butter and continue to stir-fry for about 5 minutes until the cabbage has begun to wilt, then add the chicken stock and water, increase the heat to high and boil rapidly for about 5 minutes until the cabbage has softened and the liquid has reduced to a saucy consistency. Taste and add salt as needed – how much to add will depend entirely on what kind of stock you've used. Serve piping hot.

MEAL FOR TWO WITH
Any rice dish.

PAIR WITH
Stout or black tea.

CHICKEN SKIN CRACKERS

鳥皮せんべい TORIKAWA SENBEI

These crackers are the shadow-world counterpart to edamame: shards of chicken skin cooked to a cracker-like crisp. They've got all the mindless addictiveness of edamame but none of the nutrition, although I guess they probably are high in protein. Then again, we did not come to the izakaya to lower our cholesterol, we came here to raise our spirits! And what could be more effective to that end than crispy chicken skin? Even typing the words makes my mouth water.

METHOD

There are no quantities nor a yield for this recipe because it depends on how much chicken skin you can procure. My recommendation is to ask your butcher for this – they'll usually give it to you for free. You will need about 100 g (3½ oz) per person, or 150 g (5 oz) if your guests love animal fat and have no shame (like me).

Heat the oven to 150ºC (300ºF/gas 4). Trim the chicken skin of any excess fat or bits of meat that may be stuck to it. Line a roasting tin with baking parchment and brush it with sesame oil, then lay the chicken skin out flat in a single layer on top of it. Season the top of the skin with salt and MSG. Bake for 1 hour until the fat has rendered off and the skin has begun to brown. Drain off the fat (keep it in the fridge for cooking) and discard the parchment. Turn the heat up to 180ºC (350ºF/gas 6) and place the half-cooked chicken skin back in the roasting pan and cook for a further 5–10 minutes until totally browned and crisp. Keep an eye on the skin during this time so it doesn't burn, which will make it taste very bitter. As soon as the skin is done, toss it with pepper or shichimi, then leave to cool to room temperature. It will stay crunchy for a few days in an airtight container lined with paper towels. It's fantastic with highballs (page 213).

SERVES AS MANY OR AS FEW AS YOU LIKE (SEE METHOD)

chicken skin
sesame oil
salt, to taste
MSG, to taste
pepper or shichimi, to taste

MEAL FOR TWO WITH

This is just a snack, really, so have it whenever and with whatever you like.

PAIR WITH

Very cold lager, shōchū highballs or iced oolong tea with lemon.

OKONOMI FRIES

お好み焼き味フライド ポテト

OKONOMIYAKI AJI FURAIDO POTETO

oven chips (I like skinny fries
    best for this, or hash browns)
salt (optional)
okonomiyaki sauce or similar
    Japanese brown sauce (page 22)
Japanese Mayo (page 22)
a few pinches of aonori
some beni shōga (red pickled ginger)
1–2 spring onions (scallions),
    finely sliced
1 small handful of katsuobushi

There is a quintet of toppings found on several yōshoku dishes, such as okonomiyaki, takoyaki and yakisoba, that make pretty much everything taste irresistibly delicious. These are Japanese brown sauce, Japanese mayo, aonori, beni shōga and katsuobushi. It helps that any one of these items tastes great by itself, but when combined they synthesise into a fireworks display of flavour. Considering white people's undying love for anything to do with fried potatoes, it is perhaps inevitable that we wound up putting these toppings on chips, and so *okonomi* fries are a bonafide food phenomenon in the UK and North America. My buddy Fumio (page 147) serves a version of them at his pop-ups, and at Nanban I made them with cassava, naming them *okonomi-yuca*, a pun almost nobody understood, but I still like it. As far as I can tell, using these seasonings on fries isn't really done in Japan, but they do appear on potato salad and crisps (chips), and you can find potatoes in okonomiyaki itself, so there is some precedent there. This is what we might call 'stupid' fusion – basically just a brainless mash-up of two delicious food items – but it is also stupid good.

METHOD

Prepare the chips according to the manufacturer's instructions. If necessary, season with salt, then drizzle over the sauce and mayo, and scatter over all the remaining ingredients.

TIP

This recipe uses oven chips. If you want to cook chips from scratch, by all means go ahead. But for me, homemade chips are almost never worth the effort. Also, this recipe doesn't have quantities or a yield, because no such precision is required, and besides, *okonomi* literally means 'whatever you like'.

MEAL FOR TWO WITH	PAIR WITH
Karaage 6.0 is an excellent choice (page 104).	Cheap lager or a fizzy drink (soda pop).

PEPPER STEAK WITH GARLIC SOY SAUCE BUTTER

ペッパーステーキの醤油ガーリックバター焼き PEPPĀ SUTĒKI NO SHŌYU GĀRIKKU BATĀ YAKI

One of my very favourite lunch spots in Japan was a little fast food shop called Pepper Lunch. Pepper Lunch is a chain, with over 200 branches in Japan and even more outside Japan. It's not exactly the pinnacle of Japanese gastronomy, and my Japanese colleagues teased me for liking it so much, but damn, did they do some good pepper steak. It was cheap – suspiciously so – but it was always cooked perfectly and it was also really good beef, highly marbled and incredibly tender. Of course, the seasonings were so tasty (lots of pepper, lots of garlic, lots of soy sauce) that you probably could have cooked an old shoe in them and it would have tasted reasonably good. So this is my loving homage to Pepper Lunch.

METHOD

Set a frying pan (skillet) over high heat and add the oil. Season the steak all over with the pepper. When the oil is smoking hot, lay the steak in the pan and cook it on one side until nicely browned, about 2–3 minutes. Turn and brown the other side, again for about 2 minutes. By this point the steak should be rare; keep cooking for a further 2 minutes for medium-rare and another 2 minutes after that for medium, flipping the steak every 20 seconds to form an even crust and cuisson. When the steak is cooked to your liking, remove it from the pan and leave to rest on a chopping board. Remove the pan from the heat and add the water, then set the pan back over the heat and add the soy sauce, sake, honey, butter and garlic. Simmer for 4–5 minutes until the liquid reduces slightly and the garlic infuses into the gravy, then remove from the heat. Slice the steak into bite-size cubes, about 2 cm (¾ in) wide, and toss through the pan sauce.

SERVES 2

1 tbsp oil
1 ribeye steak, 300–400 g (10½–14 oz) and ideally at least 2.5 cm (1 in) thick, patted dry with paper towels
a very generous amount of coarsely ground black pepper
4 tbsp water
2 tbsp soy sauce
1 tbsp sake
1 tbsp honey
20 g (¾ oz) butter
3 garlic cloves, thinly sliced

TIP

Use your senses and intuition cooking steak or, better yet, a probe thermometer, to gauge the steak's doneness. And remember: if you're not sure how cooked it is, err on the side of rare. You can always cook it more. If you're using a cut other than ribeye, slice the steak across the grain as you usually would; otherwise, the meat will be too tough and chewy.

MEAL FOR TWO WITH

If you serve this over rice, with an egg yolk on top, it makes a killer shime (page 144).

PAIR WITH

Red wine, rich sake, strong, dark beer or oolong tea.

AUBERGINE-WRAPPED GYOZA OF PORK AND PRAWN

海老と豚肉の茄子餃子　EBI TO BUTANIKU NO NASU GYŌZA

I had something like this at an izakaya in Akasaka and I thought it was one of the most ingenious things I'd ever eaten. Essentially, it's pork and prawn (shrimp) gyoza, but instead of gyoza pastry, the filling is sandwiched between thin slices of aubergine. I later realised that this is just stuffed aubergine, which is made in many ways in many different cultures and, in fact, this particular preparation owes a lot to Chinese cookery. So while it's not as innovative as I originally thought, it is nonetheless exceedingly delicious and possibly easier to make than actual gyoza.

METHOD

Remove the ends from the aubergine and cut in half lengthways. Cut each half into six or seven half-rounds, about 2 cm (½ in) thick. Turn each half-round into a pocket by carefully slicing lengthways into the curved side almost to the bottom, keeping it still attached along the flat, cut side, so you have something that looks a bit like a tiny hard taco shell or a little purse. Mix the pork, prawns, garlic, ginger, spring onions, salt and pepper well, then stuff this mixture into each piece of aubergine (the mixture will overflow from the edges of the aubergine – that's okay). Gently toss the aubergine gyoza in the cornflour or starch. Heat the oil in a large non-stick frying pan (skillet) over a medium heat, then add the gyoza and cook for 5 minutes on each side until nicely browned. Add the sake, water and soy sauce to the pan, then place a lid on it and steam for 5 minutes; by now, the aubergine should be totally soft and the filling cooked through. Remove the lid and continue cooking until all the liquid has evaporated. Remove the gyoza from the pan and drain on paper towels, then transfer to a plate and serve with ponzu on the side.

MAKES 10–12 CHUNKY GYOZA
SERVES 2

1 aubergine (eggplant)
100 g (3½ oz) fatty minced
(ground) pork
50 g (2 oz) prawns, roughly chopped
2 garlic cloves, minced
15 g (½ oz) ginger root,
peeled and minced
2 spring onions (scallions),
finely sliced
¼ tsp salt
1 large pinch of white pepper
2 tbsp cornflour (cornstarch)
or potato starch
2 tbsp oil
50 ml (1¾ fl oz/3 tbsp) sake
100 ml (3½ fl oz/scant ½ cup) water
1½ tbsp soy sauce
ponzu, store-bought or homemade
(page 222), to serve

MEAL FOR TWO WITH
Fried Rice with Crispy Bits
(page 168) or Spicy Sesame Ramen
Salad (page 159).

PAIR WITH
Shōchū, lager or oolong.

KOREAN-STYLE BEEF TARTARE

牛肉ユッケ　GYŪNIKU YUKKE

Korean influences are common in modern Japanese gastronomy, especially in areas with sizeable Korean diaspora populations like Tokyo or Fukuoka. Korean meat dishes are particularly popular in Japan, and *yakiniku*, or Japanese-style barbecue, is heavily indebted to Korean cookery. One of the most popular Korean dishes in Japan is *yukhoe*, which is like tartare, but the meat is very finely sliced rather than minced, and dressed with an irresistible sauce, rich with sesame oil and garlic. In Japan it's called *yukke*, and while it's mainly found at barbecue joints, it's not uncommon to find it on izakaya menus.

METHOD

Place the beef in the freezer for a 30–60 minutes until it becomes very firm and semi-frozen – this will make it easier to slice. Meanwhile, whisk together the sesame oil, soy sauce, *gochujang*, honey, garlic and sesame seeds. Slice the beef across the grain as thinly as you can, then stack the slices up on top of each other and slice through them again – basically, you are trying to cut the beef into long, thin matchsticks. Combine the beef with the sauce, daikon and apple and mix well. The yukhoe is now ready to serve, but I think it is better if it marinates in the fridge for a while (anywhere from 1–24 hours).

To serve, stir the cucumber into the yukhoe, then spoon the mixture out onto a small dish. Top with the pine nuts, chilli oil, if using, and spring onion, with the egg yolk in the centre. Ensure the dish is served very cold.

SERVES 2

120 g (4 oz) well-marbled beef, completely free of sinew (fillet or well-trimmed rump or bavette are good cuts to use for this)

1½ tbsp sesame oil

1 tbsp soy sauce

1 tbsp *gochujang* (or 2 tsp white miso mixed with 2 tsp hot chilli sauce)

2 tsp honey

1 garlic clove, finely grated

¼ tsp sesame seeds

30 g (1 oz) daikon, peeled, or radishes, julienned

¼ green apple, julienned

5 cm (2 in) piece of cucumber, julienned

1 tbsp toasted pine nuts (optional)

¼ tsp chilli oil (optional)

½ spring onion (scallion), finely sliced

1 egg yolk

TIP

This recipe calls for gochujang, a delicious Korean chilli paste. It's widely available, even at mainstream supermarkets, and I would highly encourage you to buy some, although I have provided an alternative above.

MEAL FOR TWO WITH

Cheese Crackers with Sesame and Nori (page 71) and Fried Rice with Crispy Bits (page 168).

PAIR WITH

Shōchū – or the Korean analogue – *soju* or iced barley tea.

BRAISED PIG'S TROTTER WITH A CRISPY CRUST

羽根つき豚足　HANETSUKI TONSOKU

SERVES 2

1 pig's trotter – get your butcher
    to remove any hair
2 tbsp soy sauce
2 tbsp sake
1 leek, coarsely chopped
4 garlic cloves, smashed
2 cm (¾ in) piece of ginger root,
    peeled and sliced
½ tsp plain (all-purpose) flour
½ tsp cornflour (cornstarch)
1 tbsp oil

FOR THE SAUCE

1 tbsp soy sauce
1 tbsp gochujang, *tobanjan*
    or similar chilli paste
1 tbsp sugar
2 tbsp vinegar
1 tsp sesame seeds
¼ tsp sesame oil
1 spring onion (scallion),
    finely chopped

One of my favourite izakaya in Fukuoka was a place called Benten. The food there was great, but the interior design was even more impressive – it was a bit like eating inside the bath house from *Spirited Away*. My favourite dish there was a pig's trotter that had been braised until soft and squishy, then de-boned and pressed and finally grilled. It had shatteringly crisp skin on the outside, with gooey, unctuous meat within. I spent years trying to recreate this without getting it quite right. The trotter always fell apart at the final stage of cooking, no matter how careful I was. But eventually, I learnt of a cheat, which is to pan-steam the trotter in a very thin batter, which forms a light, crispy crust as the liquid evaporates. This provides a similar crunchy-gooey texture to the Benten original, but it is more achievable at home.

METHOD

Place the trotter in a saucepan and cover with water, then bring to the boil over high heat. Boil for about 3 minutes, then drain and rinse the trotter off to remove the excess blood. Rinse out the pan and return the trotter, cover with water again and add the soy sauce, sake, leek, garlic and ginger and bring to a simmer with the lid on the pan. Simmer for about 2½ hours, topping up the water as needed, until the trotter is soft but not falling apart, then remove it and leave it to rest at room temperature until cool enough to handle. (You can save the stock and use it as a base for ramen.) Remove the bones from the trotter and cut it into bite-size pieces, then transfer them to the fridge to chill completely.

Meanwhile, make the sauce by combining all the ingredients and stirring well. To serve, stir together the flours with 150 ml (5 fl oz/scant ⅔ cup) of water to make a thin slurry. Heat the oil over a medium–high heat in a flat-bottomed non-stick or well-seasoned cast iron pan and tip in the slurry. When the slurry starts to bubble, tip in the trotter chunks, toss them through the slurry and then spread in an even layer. Leave the liquid to evaporate completely until it is completely dry and crisp (use a spatter screen or cover very loosely with some foil, because the oil will spit). Tip the trotters out onto a plate and break into chunks. Serve with the dip on the side.

MEAL FOR TWO WITH	PAIR WITH
Rice and Lightly Pickled Cucumbers with Garlic and Sesame Oil (page 47).	Pale ale or similar flavourful beer, or shōchū, soju or barley tea.

ROAST PORK

焼豚 YAKIBUTA

One of the first recipes I ever developed that I was really proud of was for *chashu*, braised pork belly used as a ramen topping. Or at least I *was* proud of it until I tried a recipe for *char siu*, chashu's Chinese ancestor, by my friend and fellow *MasterChef* champion Ping Coombes. Her version was sweeter, stickier and more complex than mine. This recipe is heavily indebted to hers. Chashu is typically braised, whereas *char siu* is roasted or barbecued; the Japanese equivalent of this would be called *yakibuta* ('grilled pork'). This recipe sort of combines both methods; the pork is first braised in the oven, but as the liquid reduces the dry heat browns the outside.

METHOD

Combine the marinade ingredients and mix well. Place the pork belly in a saucepan and cover with water, then bring to the boil and cook for 4–5 minutes. Discard the liquid and rinse the belly under fresh water to remove any scum. Stab the belly all over with a sharp, thin knife or a metal skewer, then place it in a plastic bag or lidded container with the marinade and refrigerate overnight. The next day, preheat the oven to 160°C (320°F/gas 4). Combine the cola, star anise, cinnamon, kombu and whisky or tea in a large saucepan and bring to a simmer. Remove the solids, but place the kombu into the bottom of a deep casserole and pour in the liquid. Lower in the belly with the fat side up and pour in the marinade. Place in the oven, uncovered, and braise for 1 hour, then cover loosely with foil and cook for another hour or until the belly is tender and caramelised and the liquid has reduced to a thin sauce (use a chopstick or butter knife to check if the pork is done; you should be able to pierce through the centre with little resistance). Remove the belly and rest for at least 30 minutes before slicing. Retrieve the kombu from the bottom of the dish and cut into ribbons about 1 cm (½ in) wide and 4–5 cm (1½–2 in) long. To serve, slice the belly into 1 cm (½ in) thick pieces, reheat the sauce to boiling and pour over the sliced belly and kombu. Yakibuta can also be chilled completely and pan-fried or grilled (broiled) to reheat.

SERVES 4, PROBABLY WITH LEFTOVERS

FOR THE MARINADE

4 garlic cloves, grated
15 g (½ oz) ginger root, peeled and very finely chopped
4 tbsp oyster sauce
4 tbsp honey
4 tbsp soy sauce
2 tbsp hoisin sauce
2 tbsp Shaoxing wine (or sake, sherry or vermouth)
2 tbsp brown sugar
2 tsp sesame oil

FOR THE PORK

1 kg (2 lb 4 oz) pork belly, skinless and boneless, cut into three long, thick strips
1 can (330 ml/11¼ fl oz/generous 1½ cups) of cola
2 star anise
1 small cinnamon stick
1 sheet of kombu, roughly 12 cm (4½ in) square
4 tbsp smoky whisky or 1 lapsang souchong teabag

TIP

You need to get proper pork belly for this, with nice, thick layers of fat throughout and more fat marbled in between those layers. Buy your pork from a good butcher or East Asian grocer rather than a supermarket and make sure it's got those layers!

MEAL FOR TWO WITH	**PAIR WITH**
Plain rice, salad and pickles.	IPA or jasmine tea.

BAKED POTATOES WITH BUTTER AND SALMON ROE

じゃがいものバターとイクラ乗せホイル焼 JAGAIMO NO BATĀ TO IKURA NOSE HOIRU-YAKI

A while ago, my friend and fellow Japanophile MiMi Aye – the author of the wonderful Burmese cookbook *Mandalay* – posted a photo on Instagram of one of her favourite indulgent comfort foods, a baked potato topped with butter, spring onions and copious amounts of salmon roe. Throughout the day, I kept returning to this photo just to marvel at it (and drool a bit) – it was at once rustic and luxurious, comforting yet exciting. The Ainu, an indigenous ethnic group from Hokkaido, make a similar dish called *chiporo imo*: an even simpler preparation of mashed potato studded with pearls of salmon roe and nothing else. There is something so satisfying about this combination; I love how the two ingredients balance and complement each other perfectly. The little orange eggs season the bland potato with their salinity and add that lovely textural 'pop', while the potato takes the edge off the roes' fishy intensity. I know it's just potatoes and fish eggs, but there's something really beautiful about it.

METHOD

Preheat the oven to 200°C (400°F/gas 7). Rub the potatoes all over with the oil and half of the soy sauce, then wrap them in kitchen foil and place in the oven. Bake for 20 minutes, then reduce heat to 180°C (350°F/gas 6) and continue to cook for about 40 minutes–1 hour until they are soft throughout (you can test them with a chopstick or butter knife).

Meanwhile, stir together the remaining soy sauce, roe and mirin and leave in the fridge to marinate as the potatoes bake. Remove the potatoes from the oven and leave to cool slightly, then unwrap from the foil and cut into large chunks. Melt the butter over the potatoes, spoon over the salmon roe, and garnish with the chives.

SERVES 2–4

2 baking potatoes, washed and dried
1 tsp oil
2 tsp soy sauce
50 g (2 oz) salmon roe
½ tsp mirin
20 g (¾ oz) butter
1 small handful of chives, finely sliced

MEAL FOR TWO WITH

This would be lovely with any kind of fish or seafood, and a salad or simply cooked veg.

PAIR WITH

Cold Champagne, hot sake or green tea.

STEAMED EGG 'TOFU' WITH MAPO SAUCE

麻婆卵豆腐　MĀBŌ TAMAGO-DŌFU

SERVES 2

FOR THE SAUCE

2 dried red Chinese chillies, seeds
    removed and roughly chopped
2 tbsp oil
½ leek, thinly sliced at an angle
4 garlic cloves, thinly sliced
15 g (½ oz) ginger root, peeled
    and finely shredded
150 g (5 oz) minced (ground) pork
30 g (1 oz) *doubanjiang* (Sichuan
    chilli bean paste)
2 tsp sugar
200 ml (7 fl oz/scant 1 cup)
    chicken stock
½ tsp sesame oil
½ tsp sanshō or ground
    Sichuan pepper
1 tsp cornflour (cornstarch),
    mixed with a little water
soy sauce, to taste

FOR THE EGG TOFU

4 eggs
300 ml (10 fl oz/1¼ cups) dashi
2 tsp mirin
1 tsp soy sauce

TIP

Sanshō is the Japanese cultivar
of Sichuan pepper. I prefer sanshō
partly for aroma but mainly for
convenience; it comes ground,
with the flavourless and gritty black
seeds already removed. If you buy
Sichuan pepper, it usually comes
whole, although some shops also
sell ground Sichuan pepper.

If you can't get *doubanjiang*,
you can use miso with a bit of
extra chilli instead.

Tamago-dōfu (egg tofu) is similar to *chawanmushi*, steamed savoury custard, but with a more robust texture and stronger egg flavour, akin to Chinese steamed eggs, although tamago-dōfu is usually served cold and has a distinct 'Japanese' dashi flavour. Here, I've kept the egg tofu hot and topped it with a spicy pork sauce based on classic Sichuanese mapo tofu. *Mābō dōfu*, the Japanese version, is not very spicy, with little chilli and no Sichuan pepper; in fact, it is often eaten by children. This recipe sits somewhere in the middle, not quite as spicy as the Chinese original, but I would still hesitate to serve it to kids.

METHOD

Toast the dried chillies in a dry frying pan (skillet) over a medium–high heat until they start to smoke. Add the oil, leek, garlic and ginger, and sauté for a few minutes until the leek begins to soften, then add the pork and cook for another 8–10 minutes until slightly browned. Add the *doubanjiang*, sugar, stock, sesame oil and half of the sanshō or Sichuan pepper. Bring to the boil, then stir in the cornflour mixture and cook, stirring constantly, for 2–3 minutes until the sauce thickens. Remove from the heat, taste and add soy sauce as needed.

To make the tofu, beat the eggs, dashi and seasonings together, then pass through a fine sieve into a wide bowl that will fit into your steamer. Wrap the lid of the steamer in a cloth to prevent condensation dripping onto the eggs. Fill the steamer with about 7.5 cm (3 in) of water, bring to the boil, then reduce heat to medium–low. Fold two long sheets of foil (about 40 cm (18 in) long) up onto themselves a few times to make thick, sturdy 'straps' for lifting the eggs in and out of the steamer. Lay the foil straps out in a cross on your worktop, then carefully place the bowl of eggs in the centre. Gather up the ends of the straps and lift the bowl into the steamer. Un-gather the ends of the foil and let them dangle outside of the pan so they don't fall into the eggs. Place the lid on the steamer, then leave to steam gently for 15 minutes. The eggs are done when they are no longer liquid in the middle and have a firm wobble when you shake them.

To serve, lift the bowl of tofu out of the steamer and ladle the mapo sauce over the top. Garnish with the remaining sanshō.

MEAL FOR TWO WITH	PAIR WITH
Glass Noodle and Cucumber Salad (page 38).	Whisky highballs, amber lager or Chinese black tea.

CHEESE AND ONION GYOZA

玉葱チーズの羽根き餃子　TAMANEGI CHĪZU NO HANETSUKI GYŌZA

MAKES 12 GYOZA
SERVES 2–4

10 g (½ oz) butter
½ onion, diced
2 tbsp not very bitter beer –
    amber lager is ideal
½ tbsp miso
1 pinch of pepper
110 g (3¾ oz) Emmental (Swiss)
    cheese, grated
¼ tsp plus ½ tsp cornflour
    (cornstarch)
¼ tsp plain (all-purpose) flour
12 gyoza wrappers
1 tbsp oil
100 ml (3½ fl oz/scant ½ cup) water
soy sauce, vinegar and chilli oil, to
    taste, to serve

Years ago, my friend Adam Layton, a sort of restaurant marketing ringmaster with a flair for the absurd, began a Twitter conversation about dubious fusion food concepts. My contribution was 'Reumen': the elements of a classic Reuben in ramen form or, as Adam called it, 'a steaming hot bowl of sandwich'. A while later, I decided to actually make the Reumen, and it was just about as bad as it sounds. But what *was* good was the Swiss cheese element: little fried gyoza of shredded Emmental, flavoured with a small amount of onion that had been lightly caramelised in beer. These were good enough in their own right to make it on to the menu at Nanban, only to be taken off in a few months because they took too long to make and kept exploding when we cooked them. And that's another great thing about having an izakaya experience at home: you aren't constrained by the pressures of restaurant service. Take your time, enjoy the meditative process of folding and crimping gyoza and have some sake. Dinner's ready when it's ready.

METHOD

Melt the butter in a saucepan over a medium heat, then add the onion and sauté gently for about 10–12 minutes until soft and golden. Add the beer, miso and pepper, stir to dissolve the miso and let the liquid evaporate. Remove from the heat and leave to cool. When the onions have cooled completely, stir in 100 g (7 oz) of the cheese, ¼ teaspoon of the cornflour and all of the plain flour. To assemble the gyoza, lay out a few wrappers on your worktop. Wet your fingertips with the water, then dampen the edge of each wrapper; don't use too much water or they will become unworkably soft. Spoon a little filling into the centre of each wrapper (about a tablespoonful), then fold the wrappers over the filling, and pinch the wrapper shut in one corner. Use the index finger of your dominant hand to keep the filling 'tucked in' as you crimp and pinch the wrapper to seal; use your thumb to pleat the side of the wrapper closest to you, and with each pleat, pinch it firmly onto the opposite side of the wrapper. You should get about five pleats into each gyoza before you reach the other end, then pinch that corner shut to finish it off. The cheese will melt and leak out of the gyoza if they are not completely sealed, so double-check each one, and ensure that there are no gaps or holes. Re-pinch them shut, perhaps with a bit more water, as needed.

(Cont. overleaf)

Line the gyoza up on a tray lined with baking parchment, seal-side up, so they have nice flat bottoms. When all of the gyoza are assembled, you can wrap them in cling film (plastic wrap) and keep them in the fridge until you are ready to cook, but I wouldn't recommend keeping them for much more than a day because they tend to go soggy. (You can also freeze them at this point, on the tray, ensuring none of them is sticking together when you do. Once frozen solid, transfer them to a container or plastic bag and cook them from frozen using the same method as follows.)

You will need a very reliably non-stick frying pan (skillet) with a lid to cook gyoza nicely. Stir together the remaining cornflour and the water to form a thin slurry. Heat the oil in the pan over a medium–high heat and scatter the remaining cheese over the surface of the pan. When the cheese melts and bubbles, add the gyoza, seal-side up. When the gyoza are sizzling, pour in the water and place the lid on the pan. Steam for 5 minutes with the lid on, then remove the lid and let all the water evaporate away. When the pan is totally dry, a cheesy, bronze crust will have formed – you should be able to tell when it's done because no part of it will still be bubbling and the crust will have curled away slightly from the edges of the pan.

To serve, it is best to have a plate that fits inside your pan so it can be rested on top of the gyoza in the pan. Lay the plate upside-down on top of the gyoza, then invert the pan and plate. Serve with a simple dip of equal parts soy sauce and vinegar, and a few drops of chilli oil. Enjoy piping hot with lots of ice cold beer. Beware of gushing molten cheese when you bite into them!

MEAL FOR TWO WITH

Pickles and a simple vegetable dish, such as Grilled Broccoli with White Miso and Sesame Sauce (page 66).

PAIR WITH

Strong ale, red wine, tangy sake or fruit cordial.

NIKUMISO LETTUCE WRAPS

肉味噌レタス巻き

NIKUMISO RETASU MAKI

Nikumiso is one of the most ingeniously delicious preparations in the entire world. That may sound like hyperbole, but consider its contents: miso, minced (ground) pork, sugar, and flavourings like onion, garlic and ginger. So it's essentially just deliciousness, compounded. It has many uses: you can pile it onto blocks of tofu or bowls of rice, mix it into noodles, work it through stir-fried vegetables, or just shovel it straight into your mouth, like I do. This is a classic way of serving it, simply spooned into lettuce leaves, which provide a perfect contrast in flavour and texture.

METHOD

Heat the oils in a frying pan (skillet) over a medium heat. Add the onion and ginger and sauté for about 8–10 minutes until the onion begins to brown. Add the minced pork and garlic, increase the heat to high, and break up the pork into small crumbles. When the pork is cooked through, add the miso and mix through. Keep cooking for about 5 minutes so the pork and miso begin to brown. Add the mirin, sake, soy sauce, brown sugar, sesame seeds and vinegar, if using, and cook for another 5 minutes or so until the liquid has reduced to a very thick gravy and the mixture is dense and rich. Transfer to a bowl and serve beside the lettuce leaves. Spoon the mixture into the leaves and wrap them up, eating them with your hands, along with a little shichimi, if you like.

SERVES 2, WITH LEFTOVERS

1 tbsp oil
1 tsp sesame oil
1 onion, finely chopped
500 g (1 lb 2 oz) minced
  (ground) pork
20 g (¾ oz) ginger root, peeled
  and very finely chopped
1 garlic clove, finely chopped
  or grated
50 g (2 oz) red miso
2 tbsp mirin
1 tbsp sake
1 tbsp soy sauce
1 tbsp brown sugar
1 tbsp sesame seeds
1 tsp vinegar (optional – not
  traditional, but I think it adds
  a nice mouthwatering quality)
1 head little gem lettuce,
  separated into leaves
shichimi, to garnish (optional)

TIP

This will make more nikumiso than you need for this recipe, but that's by design. It's super tasty and you'll find uses for it. If you use really fatty mince, when it's chilled, this has a consistency like a really coarse pâté, so you can just eat it on toast.

MEAL FOR TWO WITH
Rice and pickles.

PAIR WITH
Wheat beer, sake or green tea.

NASU DENGAKU THREE WAYS

茄子田楽の3種類　NASU DENGAKU NO SAN SHURUI

ALL RECIPES SERVE 2

I love to go down rabbit holes spending hours on the internet, researching one particular thing and all of its aspects and offshoots. My penchant for deep-dives is partly what has always made Japanese food so appealing to me; whether it's sushi, ramen, karaage or curry, any given Japanese dish will contain within it an seemingly infinite expanse of knowledge, detail and complexity.

However, nasu dengaku, aubergine glazed with sweet miso sauce, is not something I ever expected to spend an entire day researching. This classic dish with straightforward cooking techniques and just a handful of ingredients, turned out to have myriad variations: how to prepare the aubergine, what sort of miso to use, how much and what kind of mirin to add, etc. And then there are what might be described as '*kawatta*' (strange) nasu dengaku, which see the combo of aubergine and sweet miso reformatted as steaks, salads and stir-fries, or embellished with meat, chilli and cheese. In fact, the recipe that prompted me to take a closer look was one called *torokeru chīzu* (melty cheese) nasu dengaku, which sounded like something from a beautiful dream. This led me to several recipes that took the cheese element a step further, remixing nasu dengaku with various pizza toppings. I began to perceive nasu dengaku as the archetypal izakaya dish: hugely flavourful and hearty in its traditional form, but with an uncommon capacity for customisation. And so, here are three nasu dengaku recipes: one classic, one 'pizza' and one of my own invention, inspired by moussaka.

MEAL FOR TWO WITH
Rice and salad.

PAIR WITH
Sake, light red wine or highballs.

CLASSIC NASU DENGAKU

伝統的な茄子田楽
DENTŌTEKI NA NASU DENGAKU

FOR THE SWEET MISO SAUCE

40 g (1½ oz) miso (red, or a mixture of red and white, is my preference for this)

1 tbsp mirin
½ tbsp sugar (light brown sugar is nice, if you have it)
1 tsp water or sake

1 medium aubergine (eggplant)
2 tbsp oil

METHOD

Make the sweet miso sauce by stirring together the miso, mirin, sugar and water or sake until no lumps of miso remain and the sugar has dissolved. Cut the aubergine in half lengthways and score each cut surface in a diamond pattern about 5 mm (¼ in) deep (this will help them cook evenly and absorb the glaze). Pour the oil into a wide frying pan (skillet), with a lid and heat over a medium heat. Lower in the aubergine and cook for 5 minutes on each side until the flesh has browned and softened and the skin has become glossy and brittle. Add a big splash of water to the pan and cover with a lid or a piece of foil and steam for another 5–10 minutes until the aubergine is spoonably soft throughout. Remove the lid, boil off any excess liquid, then remove the aubergine from the pan and drain well on paper towels. Spread the sweet miso sauce onto the scored side of each aubergine half and place under a hot grill (broiler) for 5–10 minutes; the glaze should bubble and brown and fuse with the aubergine.

NASU DENGAKU WITH MOUSSAKA FLAVOURS

ムサカ風味のラム肉味噌茄子田楽　MUSAKA FŪMI NO
RAMU NIKUMISO NASU DENGAKU

1 quantity Classic Nasu Dengaku (see method)
1 tbsp olive oil
¼ red onion, finely diced
60 g (2 oz) lean minced (ground) lamb
¼ tsp dried oregano
1 garlic clove, grated
salt and pepper, to taste
1½ tbsp tinned tomato pulp or passata
1 tsp tomato purée (paste)
1 tbsp wine (any kind) or sake
10 g (½ oz) butter
1 quantity sweet miso sauce (made for classic
　　nasu dengaku)
1 tbsp plain (all-purpose) flour
60 ml (2 fl oz/¼ cup) milk
1 tbsp grated Parmesan
1 egg yolk
½ tbsp Greek yoghurt (optional)

METHOD

Prepare the nasu dengaku as per the recipe
on page 97, but stop before you glaze and grill
(broil) the aubergine.

　　Heat the oil in a frying pan (skillet) over a
medium–high heat, add the onion and sauté until
soft and golden. Add the lamb, oregano, garlic
and a pinch of pepper. Keep sautéing until the
lamb is browned, then add the tomato pulp or
passata, tomato purée, wine or sake, a pinch of
pepper and the sweet miso sauce. Cook for about
10 minutes until the lamb sauce is thick and
rich. Meanwhile, in a small, separate pan, melt
the butter over a medium heat and then whisk
in the flour. Cook for a few minutes, stirring
constantly, to form a roux. Whisk in the milk,
little by little, and cook for about 5 minutes
until the mixture boils and thickens, then stir in
the cheese. Remove from the heat and leave to
cool slightly. In a bowl, whisk a spoonful of the
bechamel together with the egg yolk, then whisk
this mixture into the bechamel. Whisk in the
yoghurt, if using, taste and adjust the seasoning
with salt as needed, bearing in mind that the
lamb miso sauce is quite salty already.

　　Lay the aubergine halves in a roasting
tin, then spoon the lamb sauce onto their cut
sides, then spoon over the bechamel. Place
under a hot grill (broiler) for 5–10 minutes until
the bechamel browns. Leave to cool for a few
minutes before serving to allow the bechamel
to set.

NASU DENGAKU PIZZA

ピザ風味の茄子田楽
PIZA FŪMI NO NASU DENGAKU

1 quantity Classic Nasu Dengaku (see method)
2 tbsp passata
50 g (2 oz) mozzarella, torn or grated
4–6 slices of pepperoni or chorizo
1 handful of sliced mushrooms, olives, peppers, onions
　　or whatever else you usually like on your pizza

METHOD

Preheat the oven to 250°C (480°F/gas
maximum). Prepare the nasu dengaku as per the
recipe on page 97, but add the passata to the rest
of the sauce ingredients. Spread the sauce onto
the steamed aubergine, then top with the cheese,
pepperoni and other pizza toppings. Bake for
about 12 minutes until the cheese has melted
and the toppings have browned nicely.

DEEP-FRYING
AT HOME

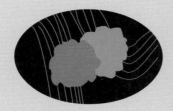

It's just not an izakaya without *agemono*: deep-fried things. Agemono are an important part of Japanese gastronomy in general, but perhaps nowhere more so than at izakaya, where the hot, satisfying crunch of fried food acts as the perfect foil to the crisp, cold refreshment of beer or sake. In Japan, and indeed much of the entire world, it is also common to deep-fry at home. Contrary to popular belief, it is not really dangerous, difficult, wasteful or (that) unhealthy if you do it properly. And you do not need a dedicated deep-fryer, just a large pan, a thermometer and a sieve.

To set up a domestic deep-frying station, first you will need a very wide and deep pot. It has to be wide to maximise the surface area; this will help keep pieces of food from sticking to each other and will also allow steam to escape. (If the food is subject to too much of its own steam it will, unsurprisingly, steam rather than fry, making the outside soft and greasy.) The pot also needs to be deep to minimise the risk of oil bubbling over; at worst, this could start a fire and, at best, it's a real pain to clean up. But you shouldn't encounter this problem anyway, as long as you're not dumping loads of food into the oil all at once – which would, in any case, be difficult and counterintuitive to do. It's easier, safer and more natural to simply lower individual pieces of food into the oil one by one.

Every kitchen should have a thermometer, whether or not you do a lot of deep-frying. They are just such a useful tool to have. For frying, you can use either a sugar thermometer or a digital probe thermometer. I prefer probes as they are more versatile, but I also like sugar thermometers because they clip to the side of the pan. The choice is yours.

However, if you don't have one and you fancy tempura, you can test the temperature by dripping a few drops of batter into the oil. If it sinks to the bottom, it's too cold; if it immediately floats and sizzles, it's too hot; if it briefly sinks below the surface, then rises back up and sizzles, then it's just about right.

Use neutral vegetable oil, such as rapeseed. You'll need enough of it to come up to a depth of at least 5 cm (2 in) in the pot, but it should come up no higher than 5 cm (2 in) below the rim of the pot. Don't worry about wasting oil – that's what sieves are for. When you've finished cooking, leave the oil to cool completely (overnight is usually best), then pour the oil through a fine sieve and funnel it back into a container to use again. You can re-use this oil a few more times – when it is noticeably darker, smells rancid or otherwise too strongly of the food you've cooked in it, it should be discarded. If you're still concerned about wastage, there are companies you can donate your old oil to that will turn it into biofuel. That's cool!

Once you've got a good, safe set-up, deep-frying is as easy and fun as any other kind of cooking. And at the end of it, you get deep-fried food!

COME
FRY
WITH
ME
!

FRIED SARDINES

鰯フライ

IWASHI FURAI

In Japan, supermarkets sell pre-breaded and frozen butterflied sardines (or aji, a kind of small mackerel), so all you have to do is drop them into hot oil to have a lovely crispy fish dinner. But making them from scratch is easy, too, and after breading, the sardines can be frozen and then fried from frozen, just like the pre-packaged ones. This is actually my preferred way of cooking them, because they are less likely to overcook. Just bring the oil up to 200°C (400°F) instead of 190°C (375°F) because the temperature will drop significantly when you add the frozen fish.

SERVES 2–4

6 fresh sardines, scaled and butterflied, with the
    dorsal fin removed but the tail fin attached
4–5 tbsp plain (all-purpose) flour
2 eggs
a splash of water
1 tbsp oil
about 60 g (2 oz/1 cup) panko
about 1 litre (34 fl oz/4 cups) oil, for deep-frying
1 handful of very finely sliced cabbage
¼ lemon
4–5 tbsp Tonkatsu Sauce (page 22)

METHOD

Gently toss the sardines in the flour to coat them evenly. Beat the eggs together with the water and the 1 tablespoon of oil until smooth. Dredge the sardines in the egg and then in the panko. Heat the oil in a very deep, wide pan to 190°C (375°F) and carefully lower in the sardines. Fry for about 5 minutes, turning the sardines halfway through, until golden brown. Drain on paper towels, then serve with the cabbage and lemon wedge on the side and the sauce drizzled on top.

MEAL FOR TWO WITH

Radish and Watercress Salad (page 34) and rice.

PAIR WITH

Sake, whisky highballs, white wine or green tea.

FURIKAKE POTATOES

ふりかけでポテトソテー

FURIKAKE DE POTETO SOTĒ

Furikake is a rice seasoning that can be made from scratch (page 221), but is more commonly purchased in handy packets or jars. It comes in many, many varieties, but classic furikake tends to stick to traditional Japanese flavours such as katsuobushi, seaweed, sesame and shiso. All of these flavours work just as well on buttery potatoes as they do on rice, and the combination makes for some absolutely world-class drinking food.

SERVES 2

350–400 g (12–14 oz) baby potatoes, washed
½ tbsp dashi powder
1 tbsp oil
10 g (½ oz) butter
1 tbsp furikake, store-bought or homemade (page 221)
salt and pepper, to taste

METHOD

Place the potatoes in a saucepan, cover with water and add the dashi powder. Boil for 10–15 minutes until fork-tender, then drain. Leave to cool slightly, then smash the potatoes with the heel of your hand or the back of a spoon so they split apart. Heat the oil in a frying pan (skillet) over a medium–high heat, then add the potatoes and sauté for about 10 minutes, stirring often, until brown and crisp. Add the butter and toss through the potatoes, then remove from the heat. Toss with the furikake, then taste and adjust with salt and pepper as you like.

MEAL FOR TWO WITH

Fried Sardines (page 100) or any simple salad.

PAIR WITH

Stout, proper German lager or green tea.

JAPANESE FISH AND CHIPS

和風フィッシュ・アンド・チップス　WAFŪ FISSHU ANDO CHIPPUSU

SERVES 2–4

FOR THE TSUYU

2 radishes
1½ tbsp malt vinegar
1 tbsp soy sauce
½ tbsp mirin
½ tbsp yuzu or lemon juice
½ tbsp water
¼ tsp katsuo dashi powder

FOR THE TARTARE SAUCE

20 g (¾ oz) pickled ginger
(any kind), very finely chopped
4 tbsp mayonnaise
½ tsp lemon juice
½ tsp English mustard
½ tsp dried dill
1 handful of chives, finely sliced

1 medium sweet potato (ideally
purple, but orange are fine, too),
scrubbed clean
1 medium floury potato (I like red-
skinned for this), scrubbed clean
300 g (10½ oz) cod, haddock or
similar white fish, boneless
and skinless
about 1.5 litres (52 fl oz/6¼ cups)
oil, for deep-frying
2 egg whites
200 ml (7 fl oz/scant 1 cup) very cold
sparkling water
150 g (5 oz/1¼ cups) plain
(all-purpose) flour
¼ tsp salt
30 g (1 oz/¼ cup) cornflour
(cornstarch) or potato starch

TIP

See Deep-frying at Home on
page 99 for tips on deep-frying.

Throughout the past few decades of fusion cuisine, there must
have been dozens of dishes bearing this name. The most famous
one in London is served at the Michelin-starred Mayfair restaurant
Umu, where chef Yoshinori Ishii serves a variety of seasonal fish
and starchy vegetables, pristinely tempura-fried and served in an
elegant *washi* cone. Of course, I made my own version way back
in 2010 – it was the very first thing I cooked as a contestant on
MasterChef. This is an updated, slightly simplified version of that
silly but undeniably tasty recipe.

METHOD

To make the tsuyu, grate the radishes very finely, then squeeze
out any excess moisture and combine with the rest of the
ingredients. For the tartare sauce, stir together all the ingredients
until well mixed.

Preheat the oven to 150°C (300°F/gas 4). Slice the sweet
potato and potato into rounds, about 5 mm (¼ in) thick. Cut the
fish into goujons, about 2.5 cm (1 in) wide. Heat the oil in a wide,
deep pot or in a deep-fryer to 180°C (350°F). Beat the egg whites
until foamy, then gently stir in the sparkling water so you don't
knock out too many bubbles. Mix 120 g (4½ oz/scant 1 cup) of
the plain flour with the cornflour in a separate bowl, then tip
them into the liquid. Mix the batter just until it comes together
with little lumps of flour still remaining here and there.

Prepare a roasting tin with a wire rack on top. Add the
remaining plain flour to the batter and mix it very loosely, just
two or three stirs. Dredge the potatoes and fish in the batter and
carefully lower them into the oil, frying in batches so as not to
crowd the pan, which will make them go soggy. As the food fries,
use your chopsticks or tongs to drizzle a little bit of additional
batter onto the surface of the crust as it forms, which will give
it extra layers of crunch. The tempura is done when the batter is
light golden brown and feels hard when prodded with tongs or
chopsticks; this will take about 6–7 minutes. Drain on the wire
rack and keep hot in the oven, with the door open slightly to let
out moisture until all of the frying is done. Serve with the dipping
sauces on the side.

MEAL FOR TWO WITH	PAIR WITH
Pickles and Sautéed Pea Shoots with Crushed Sesame (page 66).	British ale.

KARAAGE 6.0

第6版の唐揚げ　DAI ROKU-BAN NO KARAAGE

I'm calling this Karaage 6.0 because it is, if memory serves, the sixth karaage recipe I've written. And it's the best one ... so far. There are so many variations of making karaage it's hard to settle on a 'perfect' version. For this one, I've stripped it back to basics, with a really simple, classic marinade. The only thing unusual about it is that it uses a seasoned flour and white wine rather than sake, which gives a lovely fruity acidity that works perfectly with the chicken – a brilliant idea I heard about from chef Jon Sho of the excellent Knightsbridge sushi bar Kaké, as well as the food writer and karaage pop-up chef Melissa Thompson.

METHOD

For the marinade, blitz all the ingredients together in a food processor until no big chunks remain; alternatively, you can finely grate the garlic and ginger and just stir everything together. For the seasoned flour, simply stir all ingredients together until well mixed. Cut the chicken thighs into quarters (or thirds, if they're quite small) and toss through the marinade, then leave in the fridge for at least 4 hours and up to 24 hours.

To cook, heat the oil in a deep saucepan to 180ºC (350ºF). Remove the chicken from the marinade, letting any excess drip off, then dredge in the seasoned flour, ensuring that all the nooks and crannies are well coated. Carefully lower the chicken into the oil in small batches, checking the temperature periodically to ensure it is between 170–180ºC (340–350ºF) and fry for about 8 minutes. If you have a meat thermometer, use it: the chicken is done when it reaches an internal temperature of at least 65ºC (150ºF). If you don't have a thermometer, use a knife to cut into the biggest piece of chicken at its thickest point. If it's still raw, keep cooking for another few minutes until it is cooked through. Remove the cooked chicken from the oil and drain on paper towels. Karaage is juicy and flavourful enough to be enjoyed without a dip, but it's also great with ponzu, or just a wedge of lemon.

SERVES 2—4

FOR THE MARINADE

10 garlic cloves
20 g (¾ oz) ginger root, peeled and thinly sliced
100 ml (3½ fl oz/scant ½ cup) white wine
3 tbsp mirin
2 tbsp vinegar
2 tbsp soy sauce
1 tbsp sesame oil
½ tsp salt
¼ tsp pepper

FOR THE SEASONED FLOUR

150 g (5 oz/1¼ cups) cornflour (cornstarch)
100 g (3½ oz/scant 1 cup) potato starch
1 tbsp sesame seeds
1 tsp curry powder
1 tsp pepper
1 tsp salt

400 g (14 oz) (about 4–6) chicken thighs, boneless and skin on
about 2 litres (70 fl oz/8 cups) oil, for deep-frying
lemon or ponzu, store-bought or homemade (page 222), to serve (optional)

MEAL FOR TWO WITH
Rice and salad.

PAIR WITH
Lager, shōchū or iced green tea.

HAM AND CHEESE MILLE-FEUILLE KATSU

ハムチーズのミルフィールカツ　HAMU CHĪZU NO MIRUFĪRU KATSU

The 'B-grade gourmet' recipe internet is absolutely overstuffed with variations on this dish, and it's easy to understand its popularity. What's not to like about deep-fried layers of salty ham and gooey cheese? It appeals to our basest, most childlike culinary instincts. It goes by several names – fried ham and cheese, ham and cheese cutlets, etc. – but I like the fanciful 'mille-feuille', which gives it an entirely unearned air of cosmopolitan class and respectability.

METHOD

Stir together the mustard and tonkatsu sauce to make a dip. Cut each slice of cheese into four square quarters, then layer them in between slices of ham, so you have two stacks of ham-cheese-ham-cheese-ham, etc. Give each stack a little press to squish them together (the cheese will act as a kind of adhesive), then gently coat them with the flour. Beat the egg together with the water and the 1 tablespoon of oil until smooth. Dredge the floured ham stacks in the egg and then in the panko, being careful not to let them break apart. Heat the oil in a very deep, wide pan to 200ºC (400°F), then carefully lower in the ham stacks. Fry for about 4 minutes, turning halfway through, until golden brown. Drain on paper towels and leave to rest for a few minutes. To serve, cut through each ham stack to expose its gooey cheese centre and plate with the mustard sauce and salad, if using, to the side.

SERVES 2

1 tbsp Dijon or wholegrain mustard
2 tbsp Tonkatsu Sauce (page 22)
2 slices of processed (American or burger) cheese
10 slices of sandwich ham, about 120–150 g (4–5 oz)
4–5 tbsp plain (all-purpose) flour
1 egg
a splash of water
1 tbsp oil, plus more, for deep-frying
about 150 g (5 oz/2½ cups) panko
1 handful of salad leaves, to garnish (optional)

TIP

The ham in this recipe should be cheap, circular, sliced ham – it needs to be uniform in shape, fairly small (about 10 cm (4 in) in diameter) and not too thick, but not wafer-thin, either.

MEAL FOR TWO WITH

Lightly Pickled Cucumbers with Garlic and Sesame Oil (page 47).

PAIR WITH

Beer or cola.

SEA BREAM NANBAN-ZUKE

鯛の南蛮漬け TAI NO NANBAN ZUKE

Nanban means 'southern barbarian,' a term the Japanese used to describe Europeans when they first arrived in the late 16th century. The 'barbarian' part is self-explanatory, and they were called 'southern' because they first arrived in the south of the country having travelled via the South China Sea. I latched onto this term because I saw myself in it: crass and uncivilised by Japanese standards, and also, incidentally, living in the south of Japan. The word nanban was, and remains, a way of reminding myself that with regards to Japanese society, I'm a barbarian.

This word is not used to describe foreigners anymore. That would be rude. But it lingers on in certain Japanese dishes whose roots lie in this centuries-old nanban cuisine, namely that of the Portuguese and the Dutch. One of these dishes is *nanban zuke*, essentially the Japanese version of escabeche. It's a historic dish, but one that has enduring, timeless appeal.

METHOD

Combine all of the seasonings, the pepper, onion and carrot in a small saucepan, add just enough water to cover and bring to the boil. Lower the heat to a high simmer and cook for about 8 minutes until the vegetables are cooked through but still have some bite. Stir 1 teaspoon of starch together with the water to make a thin slurry, then stir this into the vinegar and vegetable sauce and simmer for another 2 minutes or so to thicken. Dampen your hands with water and rub the fish fillets to wet them, then dredge them in the remaining starch. Heat about 1 cm (¾ in) oil in a frying pan (skillet) over a high heat and carefully lower in the fish fillets. Cook for about 3–4 minutes on each side until lightly browned and crisp. Drain on paper towels. To serve, spoon most of the sauce and vegetables into a dish, then lay the fish on top and pour over the remaining sauce.

SERVES 2, OR 4 AS PART OF A LARGER MEAL

4 tbsp dashi
4 tbsp vinegar
1 tbsp mirin
1 tbsp sugar
1½ tbsp soy sauce
½ dried red chilli, seeds removed and finely sliced
½ (bell) pepper, thinly sliced
½ onion, thinly sliced
½ carrot, peeled and thinly sliced
2 tbsp plus 1 tsp cornflour (cornstarch) or potato starch
1 tbsp water
2 fillets (200–250 g/7–9 oz) sea bream (or sea bass or similar), scaled and pin-boned
oil, as needed for shallow-frying

MEAL FOR TWO WITH

Keep it classic: rice, miso soup and steamed vegetables.

PAIR WITH

Sake, sherry or green tea.

OBI-TEN MACKEREL SCOTCH EGG

飫肥天風味鯖のスコッチエッグ　OBITEN FŪMI SABA NO SUKOCCHI EGGU

These fishy Scotch eggs are something I've been making for a while, and although they may seem like another one of my own dumb fusion dishes, they're actually a traditional food of Miyazaki prefecture and date back to the Edo period. *Obi-ten* is shorthand for Obi tempura, which is not tempura as we know it now, but instead an un-battered fried fish cake found in the city of Nichinan, formerly Obi. They have a few unique characteristics that distinguish them from ordinary Japanese fish cakes: they are based on oily fish such as mackerel or sardines; they use tofu to give them a light, bouncy texture; and they are flavoured with ginger and miso. Sometimes they are plain, sometimes studded with vegetables and sometimes wrapped around boiled eggs. These are also good at room temperature, so, like a British Scotch egg, they're just as at home at a picnic as they are at the bar.

METHOD

First, drain the tofu well. Place it in a dish with a flat bottom and place another small dish on top of it to weigh it down. You can then simply leave it in the fridge for 12–24 hours, then discard the liquid and pat it dry with paper towels; or you can microwave it for 30 seconds, drain off any liquid it releases, then turn the tofu over and repeat. If you drain it in the microwave, put it in the fridge to chill completely before proceeding with this recipe.

Boil the eggs for 7½ minutes, then drain and run under cold water to halt the cooking and cool them down. When they're cold, peel them. Purée the mackerel, ginger, miso, tofu, starch, sugar and salt in a food processor until it is very smooth. Refrigerate this mixture for at least 30 minutes to firm up. Heat the oil in a very deep, wide pan to 160°C (320°F). Keep a dish of veg oil nearby. Use plenty of this to lubricate your hands, because the mackerel mixture is very sticky. Enclose each egg in a handful of mackerel mixture, spreading it out evenly across the entire surface of each egg, then lower them carefully into the oil as you make them. Fry the eggs for about 8 minutes – they should look quite brown, more an old bronze colour than a bright gold. Drain them on paper towels and leave to cool slightly before eating.

SERVES 4

80 g (3 oz) firm silken tofu
4 medium eggs
300 g (10½ oz) mackerel (about 4 fillets), skinned, pin-boned and diced
15 g (½ oz) ginger root, peeled and very finely chopped
15 g (½ oz) red or mixed miso
10 g (½ oz) cornflour (cornstarch) or potato starch
1 tbsp sugar
¼ tsp salt
about 1.5 litres (52 fl oz/6¼ cups) oil, for deep frying, plus more for greasing

MEAL FOR TWO WITH

Radish and Watercress Salad (page 34) and rice or bread.

PAIR WITH

Blonde ale, white wine, sake or brown rice tea.

There aren't really main courses in izakaya meals, but if there were, they might be recipes like these: big, show-stopping hotpots, sizzling griddles and similar dishes that are heated or cooked at the table. They have a DIY element that really heightens the sense of community and conviviality, as everyone cooks and eats together from the same large pot. One of the best things about eating this way is that everything is always piping hot, so these make great winter warmers. And there's an element of theatre to them, as well, so they're great for entertaining. You will need a gas camping stove or portable electric hob for these dishes.

卓上料理

DIY DINING

SAKAGURA SAKURAGI EXTERIOR,
WITH A LANTERN ADVERTISING ODEN.

NAOTAKA AND HIS DAUGHTER, SAKURA,
AFTER WHOM SAKURAGI WAS NAMED.

YUKIKO, TENDING BAR AT SAKURAGI, WITH SHELVES
FULL OF REGIONAL SAKE BEHIND HER.

SAKAGURA SAKURAGI:
THE STORY OF A 1970S SAKE BAR

Most Japanese food enthusiasts tend to idolise the *shokunin* of Japan – the übermensch of cooking, phenomenally skilled chefs who have dedicated their entire being to their craft. And don't get me wrong, I'm as impressed as anybody by those guys. But they aren't who I look to for inspiration, mainly because that level of cookery feels so unachievable to me. I am more inspired by Japanese home cooks, who may not have the technical mastery of shokunin, but who do have a boundless generosity of spirit and a seemingly effortless knack for seasonings and simple cooking methods that can make even unremarkable produce taste fantastic. The shokunin, the artisans, the artists – they get all the glory, all the Netflix specials and *Monocle* write-ups. But it's the home cooks of Japan who really sustain the nation and act as stewards of a different, more humble kind of tradition.

If there's any one person who has informed and inspired my own Japanese home cooking the most, it's my mother-in-law, Emiko. When Laura and I moved to London after leaving Japan, we had no jobs and very little savings, so we lived with her parents. This was meant to be just for a month or two, but right when we were planning to move out, I wound up jobless and visa-less, and so we remained in their loft conversion for a whole year while I sorted myself out. This wasn't the greatest chapter in my life story, but one thing that was great about it was getting to eat Emiko's cooking every day. At that time, she was working nine to five, but she'd still make delicious, fully from-scratch dinners every night. Over the years, she had developed her own unique kind of British-Japanese fusion cuisine, the result of having to reconcile a dearth of Japanese ingredients with the old-fashioned palate of her spry but quite ancient Japanese father, Yoshio, who had moved in some years earlier. (Emiko's mother also lived at home for a while, but by the time we were there, she had already been in a care home for several years.)

Emiko's cooking is mostly Japanese – there's almost always rice, and at that time there was always miso soup, too, but this was mostly to please Yoshio. And in true Japanese fashion, her dinners usually contained several different elements. I don't think this was necessarily by design, but she often followed a loose ichijū sansai format, with three different things on the plate, perhaps a simple protein like braised chicken or fried fish, blanched vegetables *goma-ae* (page 66) and some kidney beans simmered in dashi with sugar and soy sauce, in addition to the rice and miso soup. She would produce these meals with great efficiency but absolutely no fanfare. It's just what she's always done.

Did cooking run in Emiko's family? Not quite. Her mother, Kiyoko, was 'hopeless' at cooking, so Emiko taught herself the basics, with help from her grandmother. Apparently, Emiko's sister, Yukiko, was also quite bad at cooking, and yet both Kiyoko and Yukiko wound up running food businesses: the former, a *kissaten* (a coffee shop serving simple breakfasts and lunches) and the latter, an izakaya.

It was Yukiko's husband, Naotaka, who had the idea to open an izakaya. This was in the early 1970s, when bar culture was just beginning to boom in Japan, facilitated by the so-called 'economic miracle' that came after several decades of hard times. People in Japan finally

had a bit of money and they were in the mood for a drink or two.

From Emiko's description, Naotaka sounds like a person who never really got on with the many societal expectations of Japan. Emiko says he found it 'difficult to work for someone else', and in the span of just a few years, he held several different odd jobs, as an artist, photographer, camera shop worker, truck driver and professional gambler. It was a somewhat strange move for him to have opened an izakaya in the first place, considering he couldn't drink (he had a particularly bad 'Asian flush' reaction to alcohol) and he did not in any way embody an omotenashi spirit. 'He didn't like smiling or saying sweet things to customers,' Emiko remembers. 'He was a very, very proud person.' But it seems he was also savvily opportunistic; the reason he opened an izakaya was purely financial. It was a reliable way to make money. Naotaka's grandmother was widowed and remarried a very wealthy man who owned a lot of properties in busy commercial areas of Uji, near Kyoto. Naotaka convinced him to let him repurpose one of them as an izakaya.

Naotaka called it Sakagura Sakuragi: *sakagura* roughly translates as 'sake shop' (or 'brewery') and *sakuragi* means 'cherry blossom tree'. They named it after their daughter, Sakura, who was three years old at the time. Sakuragi was popular almost immediately. Its prime location surely helped, on a bustling road nicknamed Red Light Street, which is not to be confused with a red-light district; this is a reference to the iconic red lanterns hung outside of izakaya, an unmistakeable symbol of good times. But Sakuragi also had a novel USP that attracted customers: they sold local sake from all over Japan. This is now pretty common in izakaya, but Emiko reckons it was probably the first place in Uji to have such an offering. The idea came to Naotaka not because he had a particular interest in sake itself, but because he loved their various label designs, which are often miniature works of art, with beautiful calligraphy, patterns and striking names like 'mirror of truth', 'nine-headed dragon' or, an all-time favourite of mine, 'demon slayer'.

People came for the sake, of course, but they also came for the service – or more to the point, for Yukiko herself, who worked behind the bar. 'My sister used to be pretty good-looking,' Emiko says, 'so she attracted a lot of younger men.' In fact, she stood out as one of the only young women working behind a bar on Red Light Street; most of the other proprietors were in their 50s or 60s. But she didn't really flirt with the customers; she was just affable and pleasant, keeping the conversation 'very, very relaxed. Like talking to a friend.' Yukiko's youthful, casual demeanour was reflected in her clientele: younger and mostly middle class. 'My sister's customers were all salarymen, students and artists – these kinds of people. Not very high class but not like people working on the road. Not rough people.' It was a cheap and cheerful place; many of their customers would come early in the evening to get half-drunk before moving on to more expensive bars and nightclubs. And that's how you know Sakuragi must have been great fun – you didn't need to be all-the-way drunk to have a good time there.

Even though the izakaya business was booming, to be working in one was frowned

upon at the time. Emiko explains: 'In Japan, all these bars, izakaya, even cafés, the whole industry distinguished as *mizushōbai* – relating to water or alcohol – was always looked down on. You know, there used to be arranged marriages, and if someone was working at a bar, particularly girls, it was difficult to arrange a marriage for them.' It was considered low-class work, and what's more, Japanese people at that time didn't like the idea of women flirting with lots of different men from behind a bar. Indeed, Emiko's parents didn't approve of Yukiko working at Sakuragi, but they let it slide mainly because she was already married at that point.

We know that Sakuragi had good drinks and good vibes. But how about the food? Was that good, too? Emiko flatly says: 'No'. But customers didn't complain; they were really just there to have fun. The food was not a top priority, and besides, it was cheap, so the guests had quite low expectations. Even so, Naotaka would go to the fish market every morning to buy fish for sashimi, which he would prepare himself. Before they opened, Yukiko enrolled in a cookery course specifically for izakaya cooking, learning how to make classics like oden, yakitori and simple vegetable dishes. While Yukiko had no innate talent for cooking, she was at least able to follow a recipe, and for his part, Naotaka took a course to become certified to prepare *fugu* – the infamous blowfish that can be poisonous if prepared incorrectly. Sakuragi was never a destination for food, but it must have been at least halfway decent; my guess is that it might not have been anything special by local standards, but if it was in London, it would be one of the best Japanese restaurants in town.

Emiko was also quite active in the 1970s Kansai bar scene, as both a customer and, occasionally, as a bartender herself, helping out at her sister's or her friends' places. She admits to being 'a bit naughty', sometimes going out by herself to bars at a time when women weren't really supposed to do so. They could go out with groups of friends or with a husband or boyfriend, but bars were really still considered the domain of men, not unlike pubs were (and to some extent still are) here in the UK. 'Bars started as just men's places; women hardly went out by themselves,' she says. Men have always had several different kinds of social spaces they could frequent in Japan, primarily, I suspect, to keep themselves out of the house. 'There were bars and what they called, when my grandma was young, "milk halls",' Emiko says with a laugh. 'They were like cafés.'

Emiko took full advantage of her generation's somewhat more liberated Japanese society, frequenting izakaya, 'snack bars' (low-key, non-sexual hostess bars) and nightclubs. Her face lights up when she remembers one particularly exciting experience: 'My boss took me to a very, very expensive nightclub in Osaka to entertain our clients. I was the only girl because they knew I could drink. It was the most impressive nightclub I'd been to, with a white grand piano, and all the hostesses were so beautiful. They wore lovely kimono and dresses … and I was like that!' She says this with a laugh and a frumpy, self-deprecating gesture, as if to show she did not quite match the glamour of her surroundings.

Emiko emigrated to England in 1976, just a year after Sakuragi had opened, to study English.

She stayed on an extra year, met my wife's father, and the rest is history. I never got the impression that Emiko had much difficulty adjusting to life in the UK – she had a strong support network of other foreign students and friends – but she did miss the bars from back home. Pubs just weren't the same, not in the 1970s, anyway. 'I didn't like the pub atmosphere because there were lots of men hanging around. There were hardly any girls, and if I was there as a single girl, they would think I was hunting for men.' The lack of food at pubs was off-putting as well: 'In Japan, drinking places always, always serve some sort of food. If someone drinks alcohol without food, we think it's more likely they're an alcoholic. They just want to get drunk.'

But luckily, Emiko still found a way to cut loose and enjoy herself here in Britain. 'I went to discotheques!' she says, with a huge grin and a little wiggle, striking a jubilant 'Staying Alive' dance pose. 'There were lots of them in Bournemouth. Almost every night I was there!'

EMIKO, WITH MY DAUGHTER, TIG.

ODEN WITH 'MASTER STOCK' DASHI

居酒屋さんのおでん　IZAKAYA-SAN NO ODEN

I often ask my mother-in-law to share her recipes with me, but when I make them, they're never as good. Of course, this isn't just a cltural advantage; it's because she doesn't actually follow her own recipes. In fact, when she makes Japanese food, I don't think I've ever seen her use anything like measuring spoons or scales. Everything is intuitive, as anything would be if you'd been doing it your whole life. A lot of cooking knowledge isn't really communicated through recipes, anyway. I've cooked oden for years, following various Japanese recipes, and it's never been quite as good as it is in proper oden shops in Japan. I never really knew why until Emiko mentioned offhand that the oden at her sister's izakaya was made with a master stock, and that this is common practice – each batch of dashi is simply topped up and reheated as needed, developing more and more depth and character over time, as it picks up flavours from the various ingredients that are simmered in it. It's not hard to make pretty good Japanese food, but making *really* good Japanese food is often about experiential details like this, which often elude recipe books.

So, here is an oden recipe, but one that makes too much broth by design, so you can save it and use it again. You're probably not making oden every day, but you can freeze the excess to use later, or use it in something else – a simple bowl of udon or soba would be perfect. Just try to always save a bit of it so you can keep your oden stock as an heirloom, to bestow its subtle soulfulness onto future broths.

**SERVES 4 GENEROUSLY,
WITH EXTRA BROTH**

500 g (1 lb 2 oz) beef shin, diced
1 litre (34 fl oz/4 cups) dashi
1 litre (34 fl oz/4 cups) chicken stock
(ideally fresh, not from a powder
or a cube)
150 ml (5 fl oz/scant ⅔ cup)
soy sauce
150 ml (5 fl oz/scant ⅔ cup) mirin
400 g (14 oz) daikon, peeled and
cut into rounds about 2 cm
(¾ in) thick
300–350 g (10½–12 oz) *shirataki*
noodle nests (available at Asian
supermarkets)
250 g (9 oz) *abura-age* or similar
fried tofu (also available at Asian
supermarkets), cut into 2.5 cm
(1 in) wide rectangles
200 g (7 oz) fish cakes, such as
kamaboko; also available at
Asian supermarkets), cut into
bite-size pieces
4 eggs, soft-boiled and peeled
hot mustard, to serve (English is
fine but Japanese is preferable)
shichimi or sanshō, to serve
(optional)

METHOD

Bring a saucepan of water to the boil and lower in the beef shin. Simmer for 5 minutes, then drain and rinse the beef under cold running water – this is to remove the blood that would turn the oden scummy. Thread the beef onto wooden skewers. Combine the dashi, stock, soy sauce and mirin in a large, lidded pot that fits in the fridge and that you can also bring to the table to serve. Bring the liquid to a high simmer, then add the beef shin, place a lid on the pot and cook for about 2 hours until the shin is tender but not yet soft, topping up the broth with water periodically so it does not reduce. Add the daikon and shirataki and cook for another 30 minutes, then add the tofu and fish cakes and cook for another 30 minutes. Switch off the heat and add the eggs, then leave to cool. Cover and place in the fridge overnight.

To serve, bring the entire pot to the table along with a camping stove, a ladle and some serving chopsticks and bring back to a very low simmer. Give each guest a little bowl and let them serve themselves, straight out of the pot. Garnish with a bit of mustard and/or shichimi or sanshō. Resist the urge to drink all of the broth, otherwise you won't have the pleasure of enjoying it again! To top up your oden master stock, use the same ratios of the seasonings above, but use less of them so you end up with the same starting quantity, about 2.3 litres (78 fl oz/10 cups).

TIP

The ingredients here are just suggestions. Oden can contain many different things; this is just the tip of the oden iceberg. If you can't get or don't want to use one of the ingredients I've listed, just swap it out for something else. In Japan the beef element would typically be just the tendon – delicious if you can get it – but shin is more widely available in the UK and just as tasty.

For maximum oden enjoyment, make this a day or two before you are planning to serve it, so that the flavours have time to mingle and properly soak into the ingredients.

MEAL FOR TWO WITH

This is really a meal (actually for four!) in and of itself, but you may want some rice to fill in the cracks.

PAIR WITH

Hot sake will really complete the warming effect of this dish, or a nice cup of green tea.

WAFU FONDUE

和風チーズフォンデュ   WAFŪ CHĪZU FONDYU

SERVES 4

100 g (3½ oz) Gruyère, Comte or
   similar Alpine cheese, grated
50 g (2 oz) Edam, Gouda, mild
   Cheddar or similar, grated
50 g (2 oz) mozzarella, grated
5 slices of processed cheese
   (Dairylea or similar white cheese
   is ideal, so the fondue doesn't
   turn orange)
1 tbsp cornflour (cornstarch)
15 g (½ oz) butter
4 garlic cloves, finely grated
1 tbsp miso
4 tbsp sake
250 ml (8½ fl oz/1 cup)
   evaporated milk

FOR THE DIPPERS

about 400 g (14 oz) salad
   potatoes, parboiled
about 200 g (7 oz) broccoli
   florets, parboiled
2 apples, cored, cut into
   bite-size chunks and tossed
   with a sprinkling of lemon
   juice or vinegar
2 smoked weiners or Polish
   sausages, cooked and cut
   into bite-size pieces
a handful of cherry tomatoes,
   celery stalks, radicchio, etc. –
   whatever you like, really
2 handfuls of good bread,
   cut into 2.5 cm (1 in) cubes

Cheese fondue is not Japanese, it's Swiss. Let's make that perfectly clear, so as not to annoy both the Japanese and the Swiss. And yet there is perhaps no dish more suited to izakaya than fondue. It is, in essence, a *nabemono*: a hotpot dish, but instead of dashi or broth for cooking and seasoning the food, it's molten Gruyère. I had it in Japan at one of my all-time favourite izakaya, Kantekiya, which is now sadly closed. Kantekiya was one of the more upscale izakaya I went to, and the menu was mostly quite classically Japanese – but, in keeping with a true izakaya spirit, that didn't stop them from having a bit of fun. Kantekiya's fondue wasn't made with any Japanese fusion flourishes, but I think cheese makes an excellent partner to sake and miso, and so this version uses them as flavourings. It may seem jarring to serve fondue as part of a larger Japanese meal, but trust me, it's not – it really does go well with other Japanese dishes and drinks, especially pickles and sake.

The method for this recipe, by the way, is adapted from Carl Clarke's excellent Queso Fondue from his fantastic cookbook *The Whole Chicken*.

METHOD

Toss the cheeses together with the cornflour until the cheese is evenly coated. Melt the butter in a saucepan over a medium heat, add the garlic and fry for about 5 minutes until softened. Stir in the miso and whisk to break up any lumps, then add the sake and boil for a few minutes to cook off the alcohol. Add the evaporated milk and the cheese mixture and continue to heat gently, stirring constantly, until the cheese melts and the mixture is at a very low simmer.

This can be served in a traditional fondue pot if you have one, but don't bother getting one just for this; it can also be served in a regular pot on a camping stove over very low heat – just makes sure to stir often so the cheese doesn't catch on the bottom or start to congeal on the top. Serve with all of the dippers on the side and use forks, chopsticks or skewers to eat. No double-dipping!

MEAL FOR TWO WITH
Pickles are a must with this; you may
also want a fresh green salad.

PAIR WITH
Sake, off-dry white wine, robust
unfiltered Bavarian lager or
fruit cordial.

DASHI BUTTERED MUSSELS FLAMBÉED WITH WHISKY

出汁バタームール貝、ウイスキーフランベ   DASHI BATĀ MŪRUGAI, WISUKĪ FURANBE

You don't really have to prepare this at the table – but it's flambéed! Why would you deny your guests (or yourself) this lovely bit of theatre? I don't care how seasoned a diner you are, setting food on fire is always cool. In keeping with the Japanese theme, you may be tempted to use Japanese whisky for this. Don't do it; Japanese whisky is too nice. Use peaty Scotch of average quality – a blend will do.

METHOD

Bring everything to the table; if you're not confident in your flambéing skills, you may also want to bring a lighter or some matches. Set a frying pan (skillet) with a lid over a medium–high heat on a camping stove and add the butter. (Safety first: make sure the stove is not set underneath anything low-hanging, such as a ceiling lamp.) Let the butter foam and begin to brown, then add the mussels and the whisky and set it alight (you can do this by tipping the pan towards the flame, or you can use a match or lighter). Let the flames die down naturally, add the dashi and mirin, place a lid on the pan and cook for about 7–8 minutes until all the shells have opened up. (If any remain closed, remove and discard them.) Scatter over the spring onions, give everything a stir, switch the burner to low and enjoy. (Be sure to provide some bowls for guests to discard their shells into.)

SERVES 2–4

50 g (2 oz) butter
100 ml (3½ fl oz/scant ½ cup) whisky
500 g (1 lb 2 oz) fresh mussels, cleaned, with any open or broken shells discarded
90 ml (3 fl oz/⅓ cup) dashi
1 tbsp mirin
2 spring onions (scallions), finely sliced

MEAL FOR TWO WITH

Rice or crusty bread is a must here, to make the most of all the delicious buttery whiskied mussel juice.

PAIR WITH

Belgian wheat beer, whisky or shōchū highballs, white wine or iced barley tea.

CHEESE DAKGALBI

チーズタッカルビ　CHĪZU TAKKARUBI

When you type 'cheese' in Japanese into Google, one of the very top predictive searches that comes up is 'cheese dakgalbi,' which just goes to show how incredibly popular this indulgent Korean dish is in Japan. I remember walking around Shin-Ōkubo, Tokyo's unofficial Koreatown, a few years ago, and seeing cheese dakgalbi advertised in what seemed like literally every restaurant window. You couldn't move for cheese dakgalbi. Its appeal is self-evident: chicken and vegetables sautéed in an intoxicatingly tasty Korean chilli sauce, then pushed to the sides of the pan to make way for a lake of liquefied cheese. It's like Korean barbecue meets fondue, and if that combination doesn't immediately ring your bells, then I'm not sure you and I can be friends.

METHOD

Combine all of the ingredients for the sauce, then toss through the chicken, and leave to marinate while you prepare the rest of the ingredients. Set a non-stick or well-seasoned cast iron frying pan (skillet) over a medium heat on a portable stove at the table, then add the oil, sweet potato, carrot and onion and sauté for about 5 minutes until the vegetables have softened a bit and browned slightly. Add the cabbage and continue to cook for another 3 minutes until the cabbage has softened and wilted as well. Add the chicken and all of the sauce and continue to cook for about 8–10 minutes, stirring frequently until the chicken is cooked through and the sauce has reduced to a nice, thick glaze. Push all of the food off to the sides of the pan to make a well in the centre, reduce the heat to as low as possible, then add the grated cheese and then the processed cheese on top. Let it melt, garnish with the spring onion, then eat straight from the pan by dragging the chicken and vegetables through the molten cheese.

SERVES 2_4

FOR THE SAUCE

3 tbsp gochujang
2 tbsp sake
1 tbsp sugar
1 tbsp soy sauce
1 tsp sesame oil
2 garlic cloves, grated
1 cm (½ in) piece of ginger root, peeled and finely grated
1 tsp Korean chilli powder (optional)

2 chicken thighs, boneless and skin on, cut into bite-size pieces
1 tbsp oil
½ small sweet potato (about 100 g (3½ oz)), peeled and cut into slices no thicker than 5 mm (¼ in)
1 small carrot, cut into slices no thicker than 5 mm (¼ in)
1 small onion, finely sliced
½ sweetheart (hispi) cabbage, cored and roughly chopped
30 g (1 oz) Edam or similar mild cheese, grated
2 slices of processed cheese, torn up
1 spring onion (scallion), finely sliced

MEAL FOR TWO WITH

Make a one-pot dinner by adding parboiled *tteok* (Korean rice cakes). Or, eat with plain rice or noodles.

PAIR WITH

Lager, *soju* (Korean rice spirit) or cola.

SPICY GYOZA HOTPOT

ピリ辛餃子鍋   PIRIKARA GYŌZA NABE

I was going to include a recipe for *motsunabe*, a beloved speciality of Fukuoka prefecture, and perhaps my favourite Japanese hotpot dish. Motsunabe is made from various cuts of pork or beef intestines, simmered in a strongly flavoured miso broth along with pungently aromatic ingredients such as chilli, garlic and garlic chives. Motsunabe is a powerful dish, rich and intense, so it's right up my street, but I also accept that part of my affinity for it comes from associations with good times and good friends in Japan. If you are a fan of squidgy, squeaky animal parts, I do encourage you to try it.

   If you're just not that into guts, no worries – you can still enjoy a similarly punchy, porky, satisfying hotpot in the form of this spicy gyoza *nabe*. This recipe calls for frozen gyoza – something I always have on hand and highly recommend. But if you want to make your own gyoza from scratch, that's fine too.

METHOD

Combine the stock, dashi, miso, mirin and dried chillies in a large hotpot or casserole dish (Dutch oven) set over a medium heat on a portable stove at the table. Bring to a simmer, then pile in the cabbage and beansprouts and cook for a few minutes until they have softened slightly. Pile on as many gyoza as you can fit, then scatter over the red chilli, garlic, nira and sesame seeds. Place a lid on the pot and boil for about 5 minutes until everything is steamed through. Keep the pot at a simmer while eating, so everything is piping hot to the very end. Serve with the ponzu and sesame dressing in small, individual dishes on the side, for dipping. When all the veg and gyoza have been eaten, stir the noodles or rice into the reduced broth and polish it off!

SERVES 4

800 ml (28 fl oz/3½ cups)
   chicken stock
800 ml (28 fl oz/3½ cups) dashi
60 g (2 oz) miso
4 tbsp mirin
1–2 dried red chillies, thinly sliced,
   or 1–2 tsp chilli (hot pepper)
   flakes, to taste
1 Chinese cabbage, cut into
   large chunks
200 g (7 oz) beansprouts
20–30 frozen gyoza, defrosted
1 fresh red chilli, thinly sliced
4 garlic cloves, thinly sliced
1 handful of nira (garlic chives)
1 tbsp sesame seeds
about 100 ml (3½ fl oz/scant
   ½ cup) ponzu, store-bought
   or homemade (page 222) or
   Sesame Dressing (page 223)
3–4 portions cooked ramen or udon
   noodles, or cooked rice

TIP

Nira are garlic chives, sold at any Asian supermarket, usually under their Chinese name, *kow choi*. Please seek them out, as they have a very unique aroma. If you can't get them, spring onions (scallions) will do.

MEAL FOR TWO WITH

This is really quite substantial on its own. Some pickles might be nice, but they're not necessary.

PAIR WITH

Lager, shōchū or barley tea.

OKINAWAN TACO RICE, BIBIMBAP-STYLE

沖縄タコライスのビビンバ　OKINAWA TAKO RAISU NO BIBINBA

Okinawan taco rice is one of the most delightful dishes in Japanese gastronomy, if you can even call it Japanese. It's a local interpretation of Americanised Mexican food (a result of the persistent, and generally unpleasant, US military presence in Okinawa), which has now become popular all over Japan. I posted about it on Instagram a while back and somebody messaged me to gush about the wonderful taco rice they had at an izakaya in Tokyo, served in a hot stone bowl and mixed together at the table. I had to correct them: what they were describing isn't taco rice, it's the classic Korean dish, *bibimbap*. They pushed back: no, it was definitely taco rice – and they had photos of the dish and the menu to prove it. Never have I been so delighted to have been proved wrong, because combining taco rice and bibimbap is a stroke of genius – mad, Korean-Okinawan-Mexican-American genius. You can simply serve this in a bowl, but it's tastier if you serve it in a pan set over a low heat at the table, so the rice slowly crisps as you eat it.

METHOD

Combine a quarter of the onion, half the tomato and half the garlic along with the salt and lime juice and stir to make a rough salsa. Heat the oil in a frying pan (skillet) over a medium heat and add the remaining onion and sauté for about 8 minutes until softened and beginning to brown. Add the remaining garlic and tomatoes and continue to cook for about 5 minutes until the tomatoes have broken down, then add the beef, kimchi, if using, and all of the spices. Cook for about 5 minutes, stirring frequently until the meat is cooked through and has browned in places. Add the ketchup, soy sauce and Worcestershire sauce and continue to cook for 3–4 minutes.

To serve, use a paper towel to spread a little oil around the surface of a well-seasoned pan. Pack the rice into the bottom of the pan and set over a medium heat on a portable stove at the table. Top with the taco meat, then the cheese, salsa, spring onions, lettuce and egg yolk. When you start to smell popcorn, switch off the heat – that means the rice is toasted nicely. To serve, mix everything well and eat straight from the pan. At the end of the meal, scrape off the crispy rice bits with a wooden spoon.

SERVES 2

1 onion, finely chopped
2 tomatoes, cored and diced
1 garlic clove, grated
1 pinch of salt
juice of ¼ lime
1 tbsp oil, plus a little more, for oiling
200 g (7 oz) minced (ground) beef
80 g (3 oz) kimchi, finely chopped (optional)
1 tsp smoked paprika
1 tsp ground cumin
¼ tsp black pepper
¼ tsp hot chilli powder, or more, to taste
2 tbsp ketchup
2 tbsp soy sauce
1 tsp Worcestershire sauce or Tonkatsu Sauce (page 22)
200 g (7 oz/1 cup) rice, cooked according to the instructions on page 219
50 g (2 oz) mild Cheddar or similar, grated
2 spring onions (scallions), finely sliced
1 handful of shredded iceberg lettuce
1 egg yolk

MEAL FOR TWO WITH	**PAIR WITH**
This will be just enough food on its own, but Avocado Sashimi (page 56) would make an excellent side.	Tequila, beer, awamori (Okinawa's potent rice spirit), or A&W Root Beer, a legacy of American occupation.

YUMIKO AND MY MOTHER, ON THE TRAIN
FROM MIYAJIMA TO HIROSHIMA.

ON OMOTENASHI
(PART TWO)

When I was six years old, my family hosted a Japanese exchange student in our home for a few weeks over the summer. Her name was Yumiko. She was unfailingly sweet and warm to our family, and she tried her best to share some of her culture with me and my brother, but I was too young and closed-minded to be receptive to it. I don't remember much of her time with us, to be honest, but one thing I do remember is one day when we were out having a picnic somewhere, I fell down and hurt my knee. I cried and cried, and Yumiko came *running* to comfort me. Like my own mother, she seemed to have an innate and powerful sense of nurturing. I think the two of them had a special connection, even though Yumiko's English was quite basic and Mom's Japanese was non-existent. They're still in touch to this day, communicating by letter.

When I was living in Japan, my parents came to visit me, and we made plans to reunite with Yumiko on a trip to Hiroshima. I will never forget the smile on Yumiko's face when she saw us and she ran to greet us with huge, enthusiastic hugs. And hugs are not as freely given in Japan as they are in the United States, that's for sure.

At that point, my Japanese was pretty good, and so was Yumiko's English, so we caught up quite naturally. We spent some time sightseeing at Miyajima, then returned to Hiroshima, where Yumiko and her equally gracious husband treated us to a truly spectacular dinner: course after course of astonishing food, most notably a gargantuan flounder, carved and shaped into a platter on which its own pristine flesh was served as sashimi. The dinner also included *shabu-shabu* of top-quality local beef; I'd always found shabu-shabu a bit bland for my tastes

before, but this was something else, and with Yumiko's guidance, I also came to appreciate it for the ritual of how it's cooked. Following her instructions, you swish the meat back and forth gently in the simmering dashi, to the steady rhythm of *shabu, shabu, shabu…* until the meat is just barely poached. It was sublime. I ate a lot.

Yumiko also put us up in a very nice hotel. Her husband was a senior executive at Hitachi, so they had money, but still, it felt like too much. I got the impression that Yumiko had been feeling a debt of gratitude to us for hosting her all those years ago, and this was her opportunity to repay us. There is a word in Japanese to help explain this, *giri*, which is essentially a strong sense of reciprocal obligation. Like omotenashi, it can be a source of both happiness and anxiety in Japanese society, but in this case with Yumiko, I felt like it was nothing but a joy. It felt like the best of both giri and omotenashi, genuine and meaningful, not perfunctory in any way.

It's funny; all debts, if there ever were any, are now repaid, but now I wish I could have the opportunity to repay Yumiko. This isn't out of some stressful sense of obligation; it simply feels natural to want to treat someone who treated you. I guess that's the cool thing about generosity: it begets more generosity.

BACON SHABU-SHABU

ベーコンしゃぶしゃぶ **BĒKON SHABUSHABU**

In Japan, pork belly, and many other cuts of meat, are sold in butchers' shops and supermarkets sliced wafer-thin for use in quickly cooked dishes like stir-fries and hotpots. In Britain, pork is not sold this way, so when I began cooking traditional Japanese dishes in my new home, I would often swap out the pork belly for streaky bacon. While this works really well in dishes like yakisoba or okonomiyaki, I thought bacon was too far beyond the boundaries of shabu-shabu orthodoxy to actually attempt. Out of curiosity, I Googled the idea in Japanese and dozens of recipes came up – so it's not that weird after all! It's actually quite ingenious, if you think about it: gently poaching bacon this way is a perfect way to cook it; the meat remains supple and juicy, and the broth becomes wonderfully porky and salty as it simmers away.

METHOD

Combine the water and kombu in a large hotpot or casserole dish (Dutch oven) on a burner in the centre of the table, about 30 minutes before you want to eat. Heat gently until the water is barely bubbling, then add the sake, soy sauce and sugar. Continue to lightly simmer for another 20 minutes, then remove and discard the kombu.

Give everybody a bowl with some ponzu in the bottom. Have your vegetables and tofu prepped and ready to go on a platter and the raw bacon on a separate platter. Turn the heat up slightly on the broth so that it is still simmering, but more rapidly. Add a few rashers of bacon and enough tofu and veg to get it going, then when each ingredient is cooked to their liking, people can retrieve it with chopsticks, dip it in the ponzu, and enjoy. (Each person can mix a little bit of mustard or wasabi in with their ponzu as they like.) Keep adding ingredients to the hotpot as you go.

Over time, the broth will reduce, so top up with water as needed. Once all the meat and veg have been devoured, add the noodles. Cook them until al dente, then switch the heat off and slurp them up along with the delicious salty broth.

MEAL FOR TWO WITH

This is pretty substantial, but you might want some pickles or plain rice.

PAIR WITH

Light lager, fruity sake or iced barley tea.

SERVES 4

- 1.5 litres (52 fl oz/6¼ cups) water
- 15 cm (6 in) square piece of kombu
- 4 tbsp sake
- 4 tbsp soy sauce
- 1 tbsp sugar
- 150 ml (5 fl oz/scant ⅔ cup) ponzu or sesame dressing, store-bought or homemade (page 222 and 223)
- 1 whole Chinese leaf (napa cabbage), chopped into 3 cm (1¼ in) chunks
- 1 large leek, cut into 1 cm (½ in) slices, at an angle
- 1 large carrot, cut into thin slices at an angle
- 100 g (3½ oz) shiitake (destemmed), enoki, shimeji and/or similar mushrooms
- 300 g–400 g (10½ oz–14 oz) firm cotton tofu, cut into 1 cm (½ in) chunks
- 300 g–400 g (10½ oz –14 oz) slices of streaky bacon (smoked or unsmoked are both okay), cut in half
- a little bit of hot Japanese or English mustard or wasabi, to taste
- 2 portions fresh or dried ramen noodles

TIP

The bacon should be very briefly cooked; the name *shabu-shabu* is onomatopoeic for the sound of the meat as it swishes gently through the broth. I was actually taught to swish it back and forth three times, so *shabu-shabu-shabu* rather than just *shabu-shabu*. But I don't know if that's the norm.

YOUR BACKYARD IZAKAYA: A RELATIVELY SIMPLE JAPANESE BARBECUE

I couldn't write a book about izakaya food without including yakitori – it is perhaps the single dish most associated with izakaya. This posed a problem for me, because yakitori is one of those things, like sushi or ramen, that I think ought to be done right, or not at all. And by 'done right', I mean you need to go all in: buy a whole chicken, break it down, set up a barbecue with proper charcoal, make your own sauce and commit yourself to an evening of hands-on cooking, continuously turning skewers over hot coals in devout service of smoky, succulent, charred chicken perfection. It's pretty laborious, and unless you have a barbecue setup where you and your guests can all sit around the grill as you cook, it's kind of antisocial. So unfortunately, I figured that yakitori doesn't really fit the brief; you can't really do it at home and still have a chilled-out, carefree time.

But then I thought: that's dumb. Of course you can. I used to have that kind of laid-back at-home yakitori experience in Japan all the time, mainly with a colleague of mine named Mizō-sensei. Mizō-sensei was a strict, no-nonsense teacher of English at one of the schools where I worked. I never thought he liked me very much until one day he invited me over to his house for a barbecue. Mizō-sensei effectively turned his little back garden into a private izakaya, centred on a makeshift grill he'd constructed by taking the top off of an old school desk and replacing it with a metal grate. He'd load it up with store-bought yakitori, cuts of meat pre-marinated in Korean seasonings and various vegetables, and then we'd cook it all together while steadily getting smashed on some of Japan's worst beers. We didn't have much in common, and we spoke each other's

languages with only partial competence, but Mizō-sensei taught me a great word to describe how multi-lingual conversation can be facilitated by alcohol: 'nomunication', a portmanteau of 'communication' and the Japanese verb *nomu*: to drink. Of course the yakitori itself wasn't exactly world-class, but that wasn't the point. These backyard barbecue sessions weren't really about the food – they were about chilling out.

So the trick is to keep it simple, just like Mizō-sensei did, with the prep done ahead, and not too many things to cook. To that end, I've narrowed this section down to just six of my all-time favourite yakitori-ya items, which will provide a tasty, varied meal, but it won't have you prepping all afternoon.

A note on nomenclature: 'yakitori' technically means 'grilled chicken' and if you're being precise, that's all it is; other types of skewers are called *kushiyaki*. But in practise, most yakitori shops actually sell a wide range of non-chicken items, so the distinction is often somewhat nebulous, and 'yakitori' functions as a catch-all term for any Japanese barbecue on sticks. (In the town of Muroran in Hokkaido, yakitori actually refers specifically to pork.) If you'd like to dive deeper into yakitori and other types of Japanese barbecue, I recommend Tadashi Ono and Harris Salat's excellent *The Japanese Grill*, or you can seek out videos by 'Yakitori Guy' on YouTube.

HOW TO YAKI
YOUR TORI

There are various types of Japanese barbecues designed for yakitori and similar preparations. The ones I've seen sold most commonly in the UK are called *konro*, though actually this is just a general term for direct-fire cookers, including both grills and stoves. A konro in English parlance refers to a rectangular box-shaped grill with mesh grate laid across the top; they are the perfect size and shape for yakitori, they maintain heat beautifully and they are great fun to cook on. You can buy them online, but most of the ones sold here are ridiculously expensive, marketed as dude-bro lifestyle products rather than just a box to cook chicken on. Unless you are a serious yakitori nerd, it's better to just construct a makeshift konro-type grill out of whatever barbecue you have. This is what I do and it works a treat.

Ideally, yakitori should cook so that the exposed tips of the skewers are not above the coals, but hanging off the edge of the grill, so they don't burn. If you have a rectangular barbecue, this is quite easy to accomplish – simply push the coals towards the front of the grill and line the skewers up along the edge as you cook. I, however, have a kettle barbecue, which makes it a bit more awkward, so instead, I line up two rows of fire-proof bricks inside the kettle, about 10 cm (4 in) apart from each other, and then lay a steel grate on top of them. The hot coals are then set between the bricks, containing the heat, protecting the exposed skewer tips, and making for an efficient use of grill space. If all of this sounds like too much of a pain (remember – you want to have a good time, not stress out over your grill set up) then just carefully wrap the exposed ends of each skewer in a couple layers of foil, which will protect them even if set directly over the coals. Then you can simply grill them however you like, on whatever barbecue you have. But please do try to avoid lighter fluid – it just doesn't taste nice. Use a blowtorch or 'natural' wooden firelighters to start your fire.

These particular yakitori items cook fairly quickly, but you'll still want two zones of heat; pile the coals up higher on one side, so they'll be hotter and closer to the food. Do most of the cooking over lower heat; particularly in the case of the chicken, you need to cook it through before it begins to burn and, in the case of the thighs, the longer you take to cook it on the skin side, the more crisp it will be. The corn, hash browns and asparagus should be done somewhere in the middle, so they brown nicely without overcooking, and the quails' eggs can be done really hot and fast so they just pick up a little bit of smoke and char.

If you can, try to set up your garden furniture so you can all sit around, or very near, the grill. That will makes this infinitely more social, and everyone can get involved in the cooking, as well. Sitting around a fire, drinking beer and chomping on chicken: this is one of life's greatest pleasures. Enjoy it.

PAIR WITH

Cheap, cheap lager, iced tea or lemonade.

These recipes serve 4, generously, if all cooked together, but you can choose just a few of them for a smaller crowd. You can also add more items if you like, such as pickles, rice or simple vegetable sides. You will need short (15–18 cm (6–7 in)) Japanese-style bamboo or wooden skewers for this, which you can buy online. Make sure to leave about 1 cm (¼ in) or so of space free at the tip of each skewer so you can rest them on the edge of your grill.

The method provided here is for actual barbecuing over charcoal, which I think is really essential to the yakitori experience. You can do these under a grill (broiler) if you wish, but they won't be as good.

CHICKEN THIGHS WITH YUZU-KOSHŌ

もも肉の柚子胡椒焼き
MOMONIKU NO YUZU-KOSHŌ YAKI

Most yakitori is prepared as bite-size chunks on skewers, but occasionally in Japan I had it made from whole, boned-out and butterflied chicken legs. This keeps the skin flat, so it's easier to crisp evenly, and it's also a bit easier to prepare. This is simply seasoned with yuzu-koshō, a delicious condiment made from yuzu peel, chillies and salt. It's available online or at Asian shops.

2 tbsp yuzu-koshō
1 tbsp mirin
1 large pinch of MSG (optional)
4 chicken thighs, boneless and skin on

METHOD

Stir together the yuzu-koshō, mirin and MSG, if using, to make a thin paste, then rub this all over the thighs. Thread three skewers through the thigh, with the two outer skewers angled towards the middle as if you're constructing a paper fan made out of chicken (this will make the chicken easier to turn). Cook following the instructions on page 139.

CHEESE-STUFFED TSUKUNE

チーズつくね
CHĪZU TSUKUNE

I can't remember where I first encountered cheese-stuffed *tsukune* (chicken patties), but I think it might have been at a convenience store, which just goes to show how ubiquitous and popular they are. I am constantly surprised by people who still think of Japanese food as unvaryingly light and healthy. A few sticks of cheesy chicken ought to show 'em what's what.

4 chicken thighs, boneless and skinless, diced
2 garlic cloves, finely chopped
about 1 cm (½ in) ginger root, peeled and finely chopped
2 spring onions (scallions), chopped
1 tsp sesame oil
¼ tsp salt
1 large pinch of white pepper
2 slices of processed cheese or about 40 g (1½ oz) mild Cheddar, Edam or similar cheese
vegetable oil, as needed, for greasing

METHOD

Combine everything except the cheese and the vegetable oil in a food processor and blitz until the chicken is ground, but not turned into a paste – it should still have plenty of texture. Cut the cheese into little batons, about 5 cm (2 in) long and no more than 5 mm (¼ in) wide; if you are using processed cheese slices, fold them in half over themselves three times to form little bricks. Grease your hands with oil to keep them from getting sticky, then form the mixture into little kofta-type patties around the chunks of cheese, ensuring the cheese is completely encased in chicken. Thread each tsukune onto a skewer and keep in the fridge until ready to use. Cook following the instructions on page 139.

MARINATED QUAILS' EGGS

うずらの味付け卵

UZURA NO AJITSUKE TAMAGO

The deliciousness of quails' eggs marinated in soy sauce and mirin should be self-evident. If you can get pre-boiled quails' eggs, by all means, use them – it's a lot easier and the results are the same.

20 quails' eggs
3 tbsp soy sauce
3 tbsp mirin

METHOD

Boil the quails' eggs for 3 minutes, then remove from the heat, drain and transfer to a bowl of cold water to stop the cooking. Peel the eggs, then marinate them in the soy sauce and mirin for at least 4 hours, but overnight is much better. Thread the eggs onto skewers, five on each one. Cook following the instructions on page 139.

HASH BROWNS WITH MISO KETCHUP

ハッシュポテトの味噌ケチャップ和え

HASSHU POTETO NO MISO KECHAPPU AE

The master of our go-to yakitori joint in Japan sometimes served us this little bonus when he was in a good mood. Master always served this with just straight-up ketchup, but writing a recipe where the ingredients were literally just hash browns and ketchup felt like I wasn't really earning my pay cheque. So I've put some miso in it, which is actually delicious.

3 tbsp ketchup
2 tbsp miso
8 frozen hash browns, defrosted

METHOD

Whisk together the ketchup and miso until no lumps of miso remain. Thread two hash browns onto two skewers, so the hash browns are supported on both sides. Apply ketchup to the potatoes after grilling. Cook following the instructions on page 139.

SWEETCORN WITH SOY SAUCE BUTTER

醤油バターコーン

SHŌYU BATĀ KŌN

Soy sauce and butter remains one of my all-time favourite combinations. Soy sauce brings the salt, umami and acidity, while butter brings the lush, fatty sweetness. Great on corn, of course, but also great on pretty much everything.

2 sweetcorn cobs, husks removed and halved
3 tbsp soy sauce
40–50 g (2 oz) butter, melted

METHOD

Boil the cobs in water for 5 minutes, then remove and drain. Stir together the soy sauce and melted butter (they will not emulsify – that is fine). Roll the cobs in the soy sauce butter after grilling. Cook following the instructions on page 139.

ASPARA-BACON

アスパラベーコン

ASUPARA BĒKON

These are a little bit fiddly to make, but they're worth it. It's amazing how much deliciousness is derived from the combination of these two humble ingredients.

10 asparagus spears, no thinner than 1 cm (½ in) in diameter, trimmed of any woody ends and cut into batons about 3 cm (1¼ in) long
8–10 slices of streaky bacon, cut into quarters

METHOD

Blanch the asparagus in boiling salted water for 30 seconds, then remove and rinse under cold water to stop the cooking. Drain well and wrap each piece of asparagus in a little piece of bacon, securing them by threading them onto skewers as you go. You should have 10 pieces per skewer – keep each piece pressed tightly together. Cook following the instructions on page 139.

Most of the recipes in this chapter are what might be called shime: literally, a 'tying up' course. While rice is almost always the carb of choice in Japanese cuisine, and also the easiest way to complete a Japanese meal, in izakaya, the carb course can come in many forms. Many of these dishes are satisfying enough to have as a meal on their own.

締め

SHIME: CARBS, CARBS, CARBS.

FUMIO, ENJOYING A PINT OF GUINNESS WITH
THE SHO FOO DOH LOGO MAGICALLY PRINTED
ONTO THE FOAM.

BRIDGING THE IZAKAYA-PUB DIVIDE: THE STORY OF SHO FOO DOH

We have Radiohead to thank for one of Britain's best izakaya.

In 1996, a young indie rock enthusiast from Hiroshima named Fumio Tanga was prompted to move to the UK after seeing Radiohead perform an electrifying live show in Fukuoka. 'I was just blown away,' Fumio recalls, with some residual excitement still detectable in his voice, more than two decades later. The experience was so powerful that he quit university the very next day to work full-time, saving money to relocate so that he could fully immerse himself in the British alternative music scene. A few months later, Fumio was living in London, studying English and graphic design and, as this kind of story so often goes, he simply never went back.

Japan's loss is our gain, because Fumio now sells some of the most delicious Japanese drinking food in the country, under the banner of Sho Foo Doh – the name of the traditional Japanese confectionery shop that his late grandparents ran in Hiroshima. This wasn't part of Fumio's plan; he started off his professional life in the UK as a graphic designer, and later worked for a fashion label as a liaison with customers in Japan. When that label closed down, he began selling his own t-shirts and continued to pursue his passion for music by working as a DJ. To make ends meet, he got a job at HMV, but that was right around the time that the entire record store industry was on its last legs, lurching irreversibly into oblivion. With staff being cut at an alarming rate, Fumio realised he had to pivot once again. 'I needed to do something before it was too late. I started looking for jobs in fashion, or something I had experience in, but I didn't get any results.

I didn't even get interviews, so I was kind of freaking out.'

Serendipitously, Fumio saw an ad for Chatsworth Road Market in Clapton, which was opening just around the corner from where he was living at the time. They were recruiting traders, so Fumio figured he may as well give it a go, spurred on by a realisation that there was a big okonomiyaki-shaped gap in the market that needed filling. 'I was cooking okonomiyaki for friends at home and they were like, "f*ck, I've never had anything like this!" It was pretty popular, and it's quite easy to make, and it's cheap enough, so I thought I could do it at a stall. I applied, and I got it straight away.' The savoury pancakes proved instantly popular, and the success of Fumio's market stall led to an okonomiyaki pop-up in the back of a bookshop, also on Chatsworth Road. 'It was semi-illegal,' Fumio recalls, then corrects himself with a chuckle: 'Not semi-illegal. It was *definitely* illegal!'

That was in 2010, and Fumio has been running Sho Foo Doh ever since, as residencies in pubs and cafés across London and even at an enormously popular pop-up in Australia. Fumio's food is easy to love, full of flavour but also real personality. It's not just the same old karaage and *tataki* you find on every other Japanese menu in town; it's food that's unique to Fumio's Hiroshima heritage and his own personal tastes. The heart of the Sho Foo Doh operation is okonomiyaki, piled high with noodles and cabbage in the proper Hiroshima style and served alongside what Fumio sometimes calls 'un-classics' like sesame-crusted cauliflower, vegan gyoza and a delightful little fried sardine sandwich, which is kind of like a Filet-O-Fish, refracted through an izakaya lens.

I've known Fumio for about seven years now. We met via Twitter, back when people actually made friends on Twitter rather than just enemies. During the supermarket horsemeat scandal of 2013, we got into a semi-serious discussion along the lines of 'What's the big deal? They eat horse in Japan all the time!' This ultimately led to us collaborating on a (somewhat questionable) multi-course horsemeat dinner along with our friend Patrick Knill, a specialist in the foods of Okinawa and Osaka. Both Fumio and Patrick are kindred spirits of mine when it comes to Japanese food. We're all amateur hobbyists who became professionals, and our particular passions within Japan's cuisines are regional specialities and what's called *B-kyū gurume* (B-grade gourmet). This is a term of endearment bestowed upon the rougher, cheaper side of Japanese gastronomy: things like ramen, yakisoba, beef bowls and curry rice. These kinds of dishes tend to be great drinking food, which I think is one reason why Fumio's cooking has been so enduringly popular here in London. Okonomiyaki is not delicate food of meagre portion; it's as filling and hearty as fish and chips or steak and kidney pie. It's perfect pub food.

Of course, the very idea of pub food in Britain is a relatively recent development; Sho Foo Doh is only possible as a pub residency now because of how British society has gradually come to disavow the old, idiotic mantra of 'eating is cheating' and embrace a more European – or Japanese – way of drinking. Fumio recalls, 'You didn't see anyone eating food at the pub back then, when I first came here. Crisps, at most. I literally saw nobody eating food.' But now, things are different; at Fumio's pop-ups over the past few years, he says 'pretty much every table has food, even if they just came in for a drink. I think it's changed massively.'

Fumio attributes this change to a continental influence; he speculates that the groundwork for serving good food, Japanese or otherwise, in British pubs, was laid by tapas bars, osterie and similar European modes of drinking and dining. 'What I liken izakaya to here, are more like those trendy natural wine places where they serve small plates. That's more the izakaya vibe.' But where pubs are more izakaya-like is in their inclusivity. 'The atmosphere of those wine bars is a bit more exclusive, a bit classy and prices are a lot higher,' Fumio explains. 'In terms of how people eat and drink together and marrying food with drinks – that's what an izakaya does, but in a much more democratic way, because it's so affordable. The izakaya is for everyone in Japan, literally everyone. From rich to poor, they go.' This, to me, sounds exactly like a British pub: a place where all strata of society can feel welcome (at least, in theory).

Since he serves his food in pubs rather than in his own dedicated Japanese restaurant, Fumio says that his menu is geared towards pleasing a typical British palate. 'In the end,' he says, 'what I found is that they only wanted burgers and fries,' so of course he serves these, but with Japanese flavours. He even does taco Tuesdays and has served traditional roast dinners on Sundays. Even so, he thinks if he were to take his menu and serve it at an izakaya in Japan – maybe not the Sunday roasts – most Japanese people wouldn't bat an eye at it and would probably quite like it. 'At the end of the day, it's got okonomiyaki, it's got fish, it's got deep-fried things. And as for the tacos, I think that would be quite a good addition as well. I've never seen people in Japan eating tacos with a beer, but it goes f*cking well! I think people would be up for the experiment. The Japanese will take it, because we have a bit more of an open-minded view on food and drink.'

Fumio agrees with my assessment that the boundaries as to what can or cannot be served in a Japanese izakaya are blurry, and almost anything is acceptable so long as it fits the bill of drinking beer and having fun. In many ways, this is another thing izakaya and British pubs increasingly have in common, as British palates become more cosmopolitan and pub food offerings may include dishes or influences from around the world. A curry is a given, of course, but my local Fuller's also serves tagine, risotto, Buffalo wings, padron peppers, Korean fried chicken and schnitzel with a 'chipotle yoghurt' (ooh la la!) in addition to the usual fish and chips and pie. Fumio points out that the key to izakaya menus, as it is in British pubs, is to have plenty of crowd-pleasers, which explains why both of them have started to incorporate popular dishes and flavours from around the world.

Still, I should be cautious not to overstate the similarities between pubs and izakaya; Fumio notes that there are a few key respects in which they remain quite different. First of all, people in Japan don't tend to do all their eating in one place; instead of hunkering down at a table at the pub all night and having a single, solid meal there, in Japan, it would be more common for people to start at a casual izakaya with a few snacks, then move on to karaoke (with more snacks), and then perhaps another bar (again: snacks) before finishing with a shime at somewhere like a ramen shop or okonomiyaki place. This isn't just for fun, it's also strategic; if you keep eating all night, you can drink more and for longer. Also, the actual content of izakaya meals differs hugely, featuring more fish and vegetables than British pub grub, in keeping with traditional Japanese expectations regarding nutrition and balance in food. In fact, when I ask Fumio about what his ideal izakaya would be like, it starts to sound really quite different from a typical British pub.

'I do like eating fish more in Japan; that's just my personal preference. It's just got a bit more variation, it's a bit fresher, and they know how to cook it better over there. I don't get that very much over here, so that's why I tend to go for izakaya that specialise in seafood. And they have to have a really good selection of sake for me, actually. As for the atmosphere, I don't want anywhere that's, like, hoity-toity. A bit rundown, definitely not looking for coolness.' Fumio also mentions the importance of ozashiki, or tatami rooms, which provide a sense of privacy that allows people to be more uninhibited and boisterous. 'I do like *ozashiki*, because then we can be as loud as possible, and usually we can smoke in them. I don't like ozashiki all the time; sometimes it's nice to just walk in and be surrounded by a lot of people having fun. But if you're going with a good, strong set of friends, and you just want to have a conversation, I think it's quite nice to have your own booth. Ozashiki, seafood, good sake. Those three things. And it should be cheap, obviously!'

An izakaya with great seafood, nice sake and private rooms at affordable prices would be fairly easy to come by in Japan, but a British pub with those things remains a highly unlikely fantasy. Then again, who knows? Maybe in another ten or twenty years, the pub-izakaya divide will have narrowed further, to a point where it's not so far-fetched. After all, if there was a British pub in my neighbourhood that served a good range of sake, I would be beside myself with delight, and I don't think I'd be the only one. Even now, some people in London are lucky enough to live near a pub where they can have Fumio's okonomiyaki and chicken wings along with their craft beer or gin and tonics. In many ways, Sho Foo Doh is a perfect sort of pub-izakaya hybrid – and it would be hard to imagine a better local than that.

CRISPY NOODLE MODANYAKI

パリパリ麺のモダン焼き　PARIPARI MEN NO MODANYAKI

There are two main styles of okonomiyaki. The most widely known is Osaka-style, which is essentially a flat pancake filled with plenty of cabbage and other ingredients, covered in certain indispensable garnishes. The Hiroshima style is actually more like a layered noodle stir-fry, with a bit of thin pancake batter used to make a crêpe that sits on top of everything and helps bind all the various ingredients together – but only just.

A sort of halfway point between Osaka and Hiroshima okonomiyaki is the lesser-known *modanyaki*, which is much closer to the Osaka style in how it's prepared, but it also contains noodles. At its best, the noodles go crispy on the hot griddle, so you have a delightful textural contrast to the soft pancake itself. Like any okonomiyaki, this recipe requires a few specialist ingredients, namely beni shōga (red pickled ginger) (page 23), okonomiyaki sauce (page 22), aonori (page 23), Japanese mayo (page 22) and katsuobushi (page 23). Please do not attempt this recipe without sourcing a majority of these ingredients – it won't taste right without them.

METHOD

Combine everything for the batter in a bowl and mix well, but don't mix too much. Pour the oil into a non-stick or well-seasoned frying pan (skillet) that has a lid and set over a medium-low heat. Add the bacon to the pan in a neat row, and when it starts to sizzle, add the batter, completely covering the bacon. Use a wooden spoon or spatula to tidy up the edges of the pancake, pushing any stray bits of cabbage or batter towards the middle, so it's nice and round. Pile the noodles onto the top of the pancake, pushing them gently into the batter, then set a lid on the pan and cook for about 8 minutes. Carefully and confidently flip the pancake over and continue to cook, covered, for another 8 minutes, or until the noodles have browned nicely (you'll have to lift up the pancake with a spatula to check on them). Flip the pancake over once again, then cover it liberally with the okonomiyaki sauce; spread it out and allow some of it to drip into the pan, so it sizzles and caramelises. Remove from the heat and transfer to a large plate. To serve, top with the mayo, aonori and katsuobushi.

MEAL FOR TWO WITH	PAIR WITH
Any simple vegetable dish.	Cold lager, sake or barley tea.

SERVES 2–4

FOR THE BATTER

½ sweetheart (hispi) cabbage, coarsely diced
1 spring onion (scallion), thinly sliced
100 g (3½ oz/scant 1 cup) plain (all-purpose) flour
¼ tsp baking powder
1 tsp sugar
2 tbsp *tenkasu* (optional)
2 eggs
4 tbsp water
15–20 g (½ oz) beni shōga (red pickled ginger), finely chopped
¼ tsp dashi powder
1 large pinch of salt

1 tbsp oil
4 slices of unsmoked streaky bacon
1 portion fresh ramen or egg noodles
4 tbsp okonomiyaki sauce (page 22)
1–2 tbsp Japanese Mayo (page 22), to serve
1 large pinch of aonori flakes, to serve
1 small handful of katsuobushi, to serve

TIP

Tenkasu are tempura 'scraps' sold at Japanese supermarkets. They're full of air, and they serve to lighten and soften the batter, but this recipe will still be okay without them.

RICE SOUP

雑炊 ZŌSUI

Zōsui is the quintessential shime. It is a filling, soothing rice soup that both sates and hydrates, so all that sake you've been knocking back with reckless abandon doesn't get the better of you. It is, in fact, sometimes not really a separate dish, but rather a new course created by simply adding cooked rice into the brothy remnants of a hotpot. Like fried rice, it can be made with pretty much whatever meat, fish or veg you have in the fridge (its name literally means 'cooked miscellany'), but I like it really simple, with just eggs, mushrooms and a few tender greens. I include a small amount of passata in this as well; this is absolutely not traditional, but one of my favourite childhood comfort foods was tomato and rice soup, so this combination is irresistible to me. Feel free to omit it for a cleaner, more classic zōsui flavour, but I do think it tastes really nice. This recipe calls for a blend of both dashi and chicken stock, but you can just use one or the other. I think the gentle nature of this dish benefits from the use of real dashi or chicken stock made from scratch, but the instant versions are fine, too.

METHOD

Combine the dashi, stock, soy sauce, sake, passata (if using) and salt in a saucepan and bring to a low simmer. Taste the stock and add salt as needed. Slice the mushrooms about 5 mm (¼ in) thick, then add to the stock along with the white part of the spring onions. Simmer for about 10 minutes until the mushrooms and spring onions have softened.

Meanwhile, if you are using old rice that has been in the fridge, rinse it in a sieve under running water to remove its excess starch and break up any clumps (there is no need to do this if the rice is freshly cooked). Add the rice to the stock and continue to simmer for about 5 minutes, stirring occasionally. Scatter over the spinach or pea shoots and the green parts of the spring onions and let them wilt into the stock, then pour in the beaten eggs. Stir briefly, then place a lid on the pan and leave for 2–3 minutes for the egg to cook through. Serve in deep bowls.

SERVES 2, OR 4 AS PART OF A LARGER MEAL

400 ml (13 fl oz/generous 1½ cups) dashi
400 ml (13 fl oz/generous 1½ cups) chicken stock
3 tbsp soy sauce
3 tbsp sake
4 tbsp passata (optional)
1 large pinch of salt, or perhaps a bit more, to taste
4–5 shiitake (either fresh or rehydrated are fine), destemmed, or brown mushrooms
2 spring onions (scallions) sliced, washed, and separated into green and white parts
2 small portions cooked rice (from about 150 g (5 oz/¾ cup) uncooked weight)
1 handful of spinach, pea shoots, or other mild, tender leaves
2 eggs, beaten

MEAL FOR TWO WITH
This makes a satisfying meal on its own.

PAIR WITH
Hot sake or green tea.

SPRING ONION TUNA TARTARE RICE BOWL

ネギトロ丼 NEGITORO DON

Negitoro is a kind of simple tuna tartare, a staple of sushi-ya and casual restaurants alike. I always thought it got its name from the two main ingredients: *negi* (spring onions/scallions) and *toro* (tuna belly), but I recently read that the *negi* part comes from *negiri*, meaning 'digging' or 'excavation', because the meat comes from scraping off the skin, tendons and bones of the tuna. I don't know if that's true, but it gives you an idea of the spirit of the dish: making something delicious out of what might have been destined for the bin. If you can get your fishmonger to scrape down a tuna carcass for you, by all means, use that, but this is pretty unlikely. This recipe calls for salmon roe, but you can use other kinds of fish roe, or leave it out, but I do think it takes this dish to another level.

METHOD

Cook the rice according to the instructions on page 219. Coarsely mince the tuna and mix in half of the spring onions. Dish the rice up into individual bowls, top with the chopped tuna, pour over the ponzu and place an egg yolk in the centre of each mound of tuna. To garnish, spoon the roe, if using, to the side of the egg yolk, scatter over the remaining spring onions and use scissors to snip the nori into very thin shreds on top.

SERVES 2

200 g (7 oz/1 cup) rice
150 g (5 oz) raw tuna, ideally tuna belly, if you can get it
1–2 spring onions (scallions), finely sliced
4 tbsp ponzu, store-bought or homemade (page 222)
2 egg yolks
20 g (¾ oz) salmon roe (optional)
¼ sheet of nori

MEAL FOR TWO WITH
Grilled Broccoli with White Miso and Sesame Sauce (page 66) and miso soup.

PAIR WITH
Sake, white wine or green tea.

SPICY SESAME RAMEN SALAD

冷やし坦々麺サラダ HIYASHI TANTANMEN SARADA

SERVES 2, OR UP TO 4 AS PART OF A LARGER MEAL

2 tbsp chilli oil, or more, to taste
1 garlic clove, finely chopped
1 cm (½ in) piece of ginger root, peeled and finely chopped
150 g (5 oz) minced (ground) pork
2 tbsp soy sauce
1 tbsp mirin
100 g (3½ oz) beansprouts
2 portions ramen noodles
90–100 ml (3–3½ fl oz/scant ½–⅓ cup) Sesame Dressing (page 223)
1 cucumber, julienned
2 spring onions (scallions), very finely sliced at an angle
1 punnet salad cress
1 tbsp sesame seeds, crushed to the consistency of coarse sand
a few pinches of shichimi and sanshō (optional)
1 egg yolk

The Japanese version of Sichuanese *dandan* noodles is *tantanmen*: ramen with spiced minced (ground) pork in a luxurious yet aggressive broth made from copious amounts of ground sesame and chilli oil. A variant sees these flavours translated into a massively flavourful noodle salad for all seasons, served cold but with plenty of carbs and fat to fill you up and plenty of chilli heat to keep you warm. If you have the chilli oil and sesame dressing ready to go (store-bought is fine), it's really quick to put together, too.

METHOD

Open a window or put your extractor fan on. Heat the chilli oil on a medium-high heat in a frying pan (skillet) and add the garlic, ginger and pork and stir-fry for about 5 minutes, breaking the pork up as you go. Add the soy sauce and mirin and continue to cook for another 5 minutes or so until the liquid has reduced completely. Set aside and leave to cool while you prepare the rest of the dish.

Bring a saucepan of water to the boil and blanch the beansprouts for 30–60 seconds until just cooked, then remove with a sieve or slotted spoon and run under cold water to stop the cooking. Allow the water in the pan to come back to the boil, then cook the noodles until a bit softer than al dente – they will firm up when you chill them, so they should seem a bit soft. Drain the noodles and rinse them under cold water, using your hands to toss them to make sure you remove as much residual starch as possible. Combine half of the beansprouts with all of the noodles and toss together with half of the dressing. Transfer to a serving dish, then layer the remaining beansprouts on top of the noodles, along with the cucumber and spring onions. Drizzle over the remaining sauce and extra chilli oil, if you like, then garnish with the cress, sesame seeds and spices. Place the egg yolk in the centre and mix everything well before eating.

MEAL FOR TWO WITH
This would be good with Edamame (page 33) or a couple skewers of Yakitori (page 140).

PAIR WITH
Very cold beer or barley tea.

PROSCIUTTO-WRAPPED CRAB AND AVOCADO SUSHI ROLL

生ハムのカリフォルニアロール　NAMA HAMU NO KARIFORUNIA RŌRU

SERVES 2

150 g (5 oz/¾ cups) rice
1½ tbsp vinegar
½ tbsp sugar
¼ tsp salt
6 slices prosciutto or similar
    cured ham
50 g (2 oz) crab meat
¼ ripe avocado, cut into long slices
    about 3 mm (⅛ in) thick
2 leaves little gem lettuce,
    halved lengthways
ponzu or wasabi and soy sauce,
    to serve

Top-tier sushi is not really achievable for home cooks, nor even for most professional cooks. But Japan is full of sushi found at more accessible settings and price points, from convenience stores to *kaiten-zushi* (conveyor belt sushi) shops, as well as home kitchens. This is not the stuff Jiro dreams of – but it's still pretty tasty. What's more, I don't think it can be reasonably be denigrated as 'inauthentic'. While sushi containing odd ingredients like cream cheese or chilli sauce is generally considered the domain of Americanised Japanese food, in Japan they can get a bit silly with sushi, too. I recall one kaiten-zushi place I went to in Tokyo that served gyoza nigiri – literally an overturned gyoza on top of a little pillow of rice. Other places serve things like pork cutlet sushi and Korean barbecue sushi. Kura Sushi, one of Japan's most popular sushi chains, sells sushi topped with cheese tempura. Cheese tempura!

Global discourse on sushi is so focused on elite chefs that it's easy to lose sight of this more plebeian and arguably more fun side of sushi. Are spicy tuna rolls or nigiri topped with tiny cheeseburgers going to win any Michelin stars? Probably not. But they will make loads of people happy. Hopefully this particular 'B-grade' maki will, as well – basically a California roll, but with salty Italian ham in place of the usual nori.

(Cont. overleaf)

PROSCIUTTO-WRAPPED CRAB AND AVOCADO SUSHI ROLL (Cont.)

METHOD

Cook the rice according to the instructions on page 219. While the rice is cooking, stir together the vinegar, sugar and salt until the sugar and salt dissolve. Once the rice is cooked, spread it out in a large bowl or tray and sprinkle over the seasoned vinegar. Mix the vinegar through the rice using a rice paddle or spatula with slicing and turning motions. Let the rice cool to room temperature before making the rolls.

If you have a sushi mat, wrap it in cling film (plastic wrap). If not, you don't need to get one – just wrap some sturdy card or a few sheets of paper together in a few layers of cling film; this will be an adequate makeshift rolling mat. Lay three slices of ham down on the mat or paper, slightly overlapping so they form a solid layer of ham. Wet your hands, then gently spread and press half of the rice out in an even layer on the ham, leaving a gap of about 1 cm (½ in) uncovered along the far edge of the ham (you will use this to seal the roll). Lay the crab meat out in a tidy row along the near side of the ham, about 1 cm (½ in) from the edge, then top with the avocado and lettuce. Use the paper or mat to curl up the edge of the ham, tucking in the fillings with your fingertips and tightening the roll as you go with gentle pressure. When you've rolled to the far edge of the ham, squeeze the roll together to seal. Transfer to a cutting board and slice with a sharp, wet knife. Repeat with the remaining ingredients and serve with ponzu or soy sauce and wasabi.

MEAL FOR TWO WITH

This would be nice alongside some fried seafood like Fried Sardines (page 100) or Japanese Fish and Chips (page 103).

PAIR WITH

Lager, chilled sake, white wine or iced green tea.

CHICKEN KATSU
CURRY SPAGHETTI

カレー味のスパカツ　釧路泉屋風味　KARĒ AJI NO SUPA-KATSU, KUSHIRO IZUMIYA FŪMI

**SERVES 2, OR UP TO 4 AS
PART OF A LARGER MEAL**

FOR THE SAUCE

2 tbsp oil
½ onion, roughly chopped
1 cm (½ in) piece of ginger root,
    peeled and finely chopped
2 garlic cloves, roughly chopped
1 tomato, roughly chopped
½ banana, cut into rings
2 tbsp mild Madras curry powder
1 tbsp garam masala
30 g (1 oz) butter
3 tbsp plain (all-purpose) flour
400 ml (13 fl oz/generous 1½ cups)
    chicken or beef stock
1 tbsp ketchup
1 tbsp soy sauce
1 tbsp Worcestershire sauce
salt, to taste

2 chicken thighs, boneless
    and skin on
salt and pepper, to taste
2 tbsp plain (all-purpose) flour
1 egg, beaten with a splash of milk
    and 1 tbsp vegetable oil
about 50 g (2 oz/scant 1 cup)
    panko breadcrumbs
oil, for shallow-frying
1 small onion, cut into 8 wedges
200 g (7 oz) spaghetti

Sometimes, fusion food comes full circle. There is a famous restaurant called Izumiya in Kushiro, Hokkaido, that for over 50 years has been serving a signature dish called 'supa katsu': a combination of two yōshoku classics, crisp-fried tonkatsu and spaghetti with meat sauce. While these dishes on their own are, of course, originally based on schnitzel and spaghetti Bolognese, somehow the combination of the two strikes me as uniquely Japanese and not European. But then again, why not? While you might not find anything exactly like this on a menu in Austria or Italy, when you think about it, it's really very similar to schnitzel with noodles (one of my favourite things), or chicken Milanese with spaghetti – although I suppose that's actually more British than Italian. Anyway, it's interesting to me how, occasionally, different cultures can arrive at what is effectively the same dish through very different pathways. Breaded and fried meat with pasta is, perhaps, so irresistibly comforting and delicious as to be inevitable. Izumiya also serves a version of this with Japanese curry sauce instead of meat sauce, which is what has inspired this recipe.

The sauce recipe provided here will make more than is needed for the pasta. It is a fairly standard Japanese curry sauce, so simply have the leftovers with vegetables and protein of your choice, along with rice.

TIP

I've used chicken for this, but at Izumiya, as in most yōshoku restaurants in Japan, pork is the more popular protein. By all means, use pork if you prefer – boneless, skinless loin chops, a couple centimetres thick, will do nicely.

(Cont. overleaf)

METHOD

To make the sauce, heat the oil and chopped onion in a deep saucepan over a medium-low heat and cook for about 20 minutes, stirring frequently, until the onions have browned evenly. Add the ginger root, garlic, tomato, banana and spices and cook for a further 5 minutes or so, stirring often. Add the butter and let it melt into the mixture. Add the flour and continue to cook for 5 minutes, stirring well to make a roux. Pour in the stock along with the ketchup, soy sauce and Worcestershire sauce, increase the heat to medium–high and bring to a high simmer. Simmer for 5 more minutes, stirring well and scraping the bottom of the pan to ensure nothing is catching. Remove from the heat, then purée with a blender or immersion blender until very, very smooth (if you really want that silky Japanese curry texture, pass the sauce through a fine sieve as well). Taste and adjust the seasoning with salt as needed.

Season the chicken thighs well with salt and pepper, then dredge in the flour. Coat them in the beaten egg mixture, allowing them to soak for a minute or so to bond with the flour and form a glue. Toss the chicken in the panko until well coated. Heat a little oil (about 5 mm (¼ in) in depth) in a large frying pan (skillet) over a medium heat. Add the onion and fry until soft and lightly browned, about 8 minutes, then remove with a slotted spoon and stir into the curry sauce. Lay the breaded chicken in the oil, and cook for about 5–6 minutes on each side until golden.

Meanwhile, bring the sauce back to a low simmer and bring a large pan of water to a rolling boil. You are aiming for the pasta to be ready just after the chicken. Place the spaghetti in the boiling water and cook until al dente, about 8–10 minutes. When the chicken is cooked, remove from the oil and drain on paper towels or a wire rack, then leave to rest briefly as you drain the pasta. Transfer the pasta to a large serving bowl and pour over about half of the sauce, then slice the chicken and place on top.

MEAL FOR TWO WITH	PAIR WITH
This is a meal on its own, but it would be nice with a light, leafy salad with Wafu Dressing (page 222).	Fruity white wine or iced black tea.

FRIED RICE WITH CRISPY BITS

カリカリお焦げの焼き飯　KARIKARI OKOGE NO YAKIMESHI

I started cooking fried rice shortly after I first ate it at Izumi's restaurant in Milwaukee, about 20 years ago. I now make pretty good fried rice, but it still isn't as good as Izumi's; though perhaps no fried rice ever can be. Of course, fried rice is a personal thing – some people like it fluffy and relatively plain, some people like it dense and highly seasoned. I like it in pretty much all its forms, but I especially like it when the rice is left to sizzle in the pan, untouched, so it forms little crispy bits. This gives it a nice textural contrast as well as a lovely scorched rice aroma.

METHOD

This is a very quickly cooked dish, so make sure all your prep is done and laid out before you start cooking. Heat half the oil in a very reliable non-stick frying pan (skillet) or well-seasoned wok over very high heat, and add the prawns and onions. Stir-fry for 3–4 minutes, then clear a space in the centre of the pan and pour in the eggs. Scramble the eggs, then remove everything from the pan and set aside. Add the remaining oil to the pan, then add the mushrooms, garlic and spring onions. Stir-fry for a minute or so, then add the rice and a little splash of water. Break up the rice with your spatula so there are no clumps, then reduce heat to medium and add all of the seasonings, as well as the beni shōga. Fold in the prawns, eggs and onions, then gently press the rice down into the pan to maximise crispiness, then leave to fry for about 5 minutes, without stirring. After a while, you should be able to smell a nutty, popcorn-like aroma coming from the pan – this means the rice is toasting nicely. Once you start to smell this, continue to fry the rice for another couple of minutes, then tip it out onto a plate and enjoy.

SERVES 2

2 tbsp oil
200 g (7 oz) raw, peeled and deveined king prawns
½ onion, finely diced
2 eggs, beaten
50–60 g (2–2½ oz) shiitake (de-stemmed) or chestnut mushrooms, finely sliced
2 garlic cloves, finely chopped
2 spring onions (scallions), roughly chopped
2 large portions cooked and chilled rice (from about 200 g (7 oz/1 cup) uncooked weight)
1½ tbsp soy sauce
1 tbsp mirin
1 tbsp sake
1 tbsp sesame oil
¼ tsp dashi powder
white pepper, to taste
20–30 g (¾–1 oz) beni shōga (red pickled ginger), coarsely chopped

MEAL FOR TWO WITH
This is a good meal by itself.

PAIR WITH
Beer or barley tea.

TIP
This recipe uses prawns – my favourite. You can leave them out for a vegetarian version, or use a different protein, if you prefer. The process is the same.

KEEMA CURRY RICE GRATIN

キーマカレードリア KĪMA KARĒ DORIA

One of the most famous foods from Kitakyushu, where I lived in Japan, is yaki-curry: an extraordinarily crowd-pleasing gratin of Japanese curry and rice, usually with a runny egg in the middle. I later discovered that this is an offshoot of another yōshoku dish called *doria* – a Japanese version of the very old-school French classic *riz au gratin* – in which Japanese rice is smothered in various sauces and ingredients, then topped with cheese and baked until gooey and golden brown. It is utterly, utterly delicious, as suitable for a family meal as it is for a night of unbridled boozing.

METHOD

Cook the rice according to the instructions on page 219. Preheat the oven to 180ºC (350°F/gas 6) and butter a gratin dish or small baking dish about 20 cm (8 in) in diameter and at least 2.5 cm (1 in) deep.

Melt the knob of butter in a frying pan (skillet) over a medium heat and add the onions. Cook for about 8 minutes until the onions soften and brown lightly, then add the garlic, ginger root and minced beef, and sauté for about 10 minutes, stirring occasionally, until the mixture has browned and cooked through. Stir in the spices and tomato purée and cook for another 2–3 minutes, stirring constantly. Add the tinned tomatoes, ketchup, soy sauce and Worcestershire sauce and cook for a further 10 minutes or so for all of the flavours to come together. Stir in the peas and remove from heat.

Pack the rice into the bottom of the prepared dish in an even layer. Top with the curry, then use a spoon to make a little hollow in the curry and rice in the centre of the dish. Crack the egg into this hollow, then cover everything with cheese. Transfer to the oven and bake for 15–18 minutes until the cheese has melted and the egg white has set. Scatter over the fried onions, if using, and enjoy piping hot. Serve with plenty of pickles on the side.

SERVES 2–4

200 g (7 oz/1 cup) rice
1 knob of butter, plus a little more, for greasing
1 small onion, diced
1 garlic clove, grated
1 cm (½ in) ginger root, peeled and finely chopped
200 g (7 oz) minced (ground) beef
2 tbsp hot curry powder
1 tbsp garam masala
a few pinches of black pepper
1 tbsp tomato purée (paste)
400 g (14 oz) tin of tomatoes, chopped
1 tbsp ketchup
2 tbsp soy sauce
½ tsp Worcestershire sauce
50 g (2 oz) frozen peas
1 egg
100 g (3½ oz) mozzarella or similar mild cheese, grated
1 handful of crispy fried onions (optional)
beni shōga (red pickled ginger) or fukujin pickles, to taste

MEAL FOR TWO WITH
Salad or similar; the Lightly Pickled Cucumbers with Garlic and Sesame Oil (page 47) are nice.

PAIR WITH
Lager or black tea.

FISH FINGER HAND ROLLS

フィッシュフィンガー手巻き　FISSHU FINGĀ TEMAKI

**MAKES 8 LITTLE HAND ROLLS;
SERVES 2–4**

200 g (7 oz/1 cup) rice
2 tbsp vinegar
2 tsp sugar
¼ tsp salt
40–50 g (2 oz) daikon, peeled,
    or radishes
iced water
8 fish fingers
Japanese Mayo (page 22) or
    Tartare Sauce (page 103)
1 handful of pea shoots
2 sheets nori
soy sauce, as needed
wasabi, as needed

This dish was inspired by recipes by two cooks that I, and many others, idolise: Ivan Orkin and Nigella Lawson. In Orkin's excellent *The Gaijin Cookbook*, he provides a guide for hosting a *temaki* party, a great way to enjoy sushi at home that requires no particular skill or technique. You simply bring cooked and seasoned sushi rice, some choice fillings, nori and condiments to the table, and let everybody assemble their own little temaki, or hand rolls. It's brilliant – we did this a few days after Christmas when I was craving Japanese food but had no fresh fish in the house. Enter Nigella. Lately, everybody has been talking about her fish finger *bhorta*, a recipe she borrowed (with permission) from the journalist and activist Ash Sarkar. Basically, it's a sort of dry curry made with smashed-up fish fingers; the kind of thing that's so ingenious yet so simple that it has made us all wonder why we haven't been making it our whole lives. Indeed, it's certainly got me thinking why I've never utilised fish fingers in anything more interesting than a sandwich before. This must have been in the back of my mind when I reached for them to use in our temaki party. If you think about it, it makes sense; fried seafood is no stranger to sushi, after all. I texted my friend Yuki (of Bar Yuki fame, page 8) a photo of my invention, expecting her to laugh at me. Instead, she simply replied, 'Yummy, it's like *ebi-fry temaki*!' – referring to the perennial favourite, panko-crusted fried prawns (shrimp). So there you have it: fish fingers are just the poor man's ebi-fry, and they make a killer temaki.

(Cont. overleaf)

METHOD

Cook the rice according to the instructions on page 219. While the rice is cooking, stir together the vinegar, sugar and salt until the sugar and salt dissolve. Once the rice is cooked, spread it out in a large bowl or tray and sprinkle over the seasoned vinegar. Mix the vinegar through the rice using a rice paddle or spatula with slicing and turning motions. Let the rice cool to room temperature before making the rolls. Slice the daikon or radishes very thinly – use a mandoline if you have one, and if you don't, use a very sharp knife and take your time. Cut down the length of the daikon, rather than across, so you have rectangles rather than circles. Stack the slices of daikon up and cut them again into very thin shreds. Transfer this to a bowl of cold water with a few ice cubes and leave to soak for about 20 minutes (if you don't have ice, just put the bowl in the fridge).

Cook the fish fingers according to the manufacturers' instructions, but I would recommend giving them a few minutes extra to get really crisp. Drain the daikon and dry it well with paper towels. Toast the nori by waving each sheet back and forth 15–20 cm (6–8 in) over an open flame on the hob, for about 30 seconds each. Cut each sheet into four squares. Bring everything to the table along with chopsticks, side plates and little dip pots. To assemble, hold a piece of nori in your hand, then use the chopsticks to pile in a little mound of rice, then top with the mayo or tartare sauce, then some daikon and pea shoots, then the fish fingers. Wrap it up like something halfway between a taco and a burrito, and eat with your hands. Dip it in the soy sauce and a little wasabi with each bite.

MEAL FOR TWO WITH	PAIR WITH
Miso soup and some simply prepared vegetables would make this a lovely meal.	Lager, chilled sake, white wine or iced green tea.

UDON CARBONARA WITH BACON TEMPURA

うどんカルボナーラのベーコン天ぷら乗せ   UDON KARUBONĀRA NO BĒKON TENPURA NOSE

SERVES 2

3 eggs

2 tbsp tsuyu, store-bought or homemade (page 220)

1 tbsp soy sauce

about 1 litre (34 fl oz/4 cups) oil, for frying and a little more for greasing

100 ml (3½ fl oz/scant ½ cup) very cold sparkling water

75 g (2½ oz/scant ⅔ cup) plus 1 tbsp plain (all-purpose) flour

15 g (½ oz) cornflour (cornstarch) or potato starch

2 slices of thick-cut back bacon or 4 slices of streaky bacon

2 portions udon noodles

30 g (1 oz) cold butter, cut into two pats

20 g (¾ oz) Parmesan, grated

quite a lot of freshly ground black pepper

1 spring onion (scallion), finely sliced

TIP

Make sure you have all your mise en place ready to go for this before you start frying the bacon and boiling the noodles. If you are still slicing spring onions or grating cheese when they're done, the noodles will stick together and the tempura will lose its crunch.

I think I first heard about udon carbonara from Lizzie Mabbott's excellent cookbook *Chinatown Kitchen*. It is, of course, an ingenious idea – the creamy sauce is a perfect match for the pudgy chew of udon. Years later I tried an outstanding version at Udon Shin in Tokyo, with the butter, egg and cheese separate until you mix it up, and an enormous slice of tempura-fried thick-cut bacon on the side. I repeat: tempura-fried bacon. This is why I love Japan.

METHOD

Beat one egg with the tsuyu and soy sauce and divide it into two pasta bowls. Lightly oil a couple of very small containers. Separate the other eggs, and transfer the yolks to the oiled containers. Reserve the egg whites for the tempura batter.

Heat the oil in a wide, deep pot or deep fryer to 180°C (350°F). Test the temperature by dripping a few drops of batter into the oil. If it sinks, it's too cold; if it immediately floats and sizzles, it's too hot; if it briefly sinks below the surface, then rises back up and sizzles, it's just about right.

Beat the egg whites until foamy, then stir in the sparkling water, gently, so you don't knock out too many bubbles. Mix 75 g (2½ oz/scant ⅔ cup) of the plain flour with the cornflour in a separate bowl, then tip them into the liquid. Mix the batter just until it comes together. Scatter the remaining flour over the surface, but don't stir it in.

Get a saucepan full of boiling water on the go and prepare a roasting tin with a wire rack on top. Dredge the bacon slices in the batter and carefully lower them into the oil. As they fry, use your chopsticks or tongs to drizzle a little extra batter onto the surface of the crust as it forms, which will give it extra layers of crunch. The tempura is done when the batter is light golden brown and feels hard when prodded with tongs or chopsticks; this will take about 5–6 minutes. Drain on the wire rack.

As soon as the bacon is done, boil the noodles until cooked but not soft. Drain the noodles, then divide into the two bowls with the egg-tsuyu mixture. Mix the noodles briefly, then top with the separated egg yolks, butter, cheese, pepper, spring onions and bacon. Mix it all up before eating.

MEAL FOR TWO WITH	**PAIR WITH**
You'll have tempura batter leftover, so fry asparagus, green beans or broccoli to complete the meal.	White or rose wine, Belgian blonde ale or crisp, acidic sake.

CHICKEN RICE

かしわ飯　KASHIWA MESHI

Kashiwa is a regional word for chicken used in parts of southwestern Japan, perhaps most famously in a northern Kyushu speciality, *kashiwa meshi*: chicken rice. Kashiwa meshi has several variants: one is like a pilaf studded with braised chicken and vegetables, and the other, served as a bento, is plain rice simply topped with minced chicken, shredded egg and nori. This recipe is based on the former, but with the egg and nori, too.

METHOD

Pour the oil into a saucepan with a snug-fitting lid (you'll be cooking the rice in here along with everything else, so make sure it's the right size, not too large nor too small). Place over a medium–high heat, then add the chicken and fry for 7–8 minutes, flipping halfway through, until just cooked through and browned. Remove the chicken, then tip in the egg and scramble it, then remove that as well. Leave the pan to cool, and tip out any excess oil. If using burdock, prepare a small bowl of water with a splash of vinegar in it. Peel the burdock and cut it into fine shreds, using a motion as if you were sharpening a pencil. Transfer the burdock shavings to the vinegared water to keep them from discolouring.

Combine the rice, water and all seasonings in the saucepan. Scatter over the vegetables, then place the chicken thigh on top, and bring the liquid to the boil over a high heat, with the lid off. As soon as the liquid is boiling, reduce heat to low and place a lid on the pan and cook for 15 minutes. Remove from the heat and let stand for 5 minutes. Take the chicken off the top of the rice, and fluff the rice and vegetables to mix. Place the lid back on the pan. Shred the chicken with your hands or a couple of forks, then stir through the rice along with the scrambled egg. Garnish with the shredded nori.

SERVES 2

1 tbsp oil
1 chicken thigh, boneless
1 egg, beaten
10–12 cm (4–5 in) chunk of burdock root (optional)
200 g (7 oz/1 cup) rice, washed
200 ml (7 fl oz/scant 1 cup) water
a little vinegar (optional)
2 tbsp soy sauce
2 tbsp sake
2 tbsp mirin
1 tsp katsuo dashi powder
½ small carrot, cut into a small dice
2 shiitake mushrooms, destemmed and sliced about 3 mm (⅛ in) thick
¼ sheet of nori, shredded

MEAL FOR TWO WITH

Any simple vegetable dish and some miso soup would make this a tasty meal.

PAIR WITH

Hot shōchū or green tea.

TIP

This recipe calls for burdock root, or *gobō*, which is sold at Asian supermarkets. Jerusalem artichokes are an adequate substitute.

FLUFFY-CREAMY OMURICE

ふわとろオムライス   FUWA-TORO OMURAISU

**SERVES 1–2, OR UP TO 4
AS PART OF A LARGER MEAL**

FOR THE SAUCE

100 ml (3½ fl oz/scant ½ cup)
    ruby port
100 ml (3½ fl oz/scant ½ cup) real
    beef stock (not from a cube)
1 tbsp tomato purée (paste)
4 tbsp ketchup
1 tbsp soy sauce
1 dash of Worcestershire sauce
15 g (½ oz) butter

FOR THE FRIED RICE

1 knob of butter
1 banana shallot or small onion, diced
60 g (2 oz) mushrooms (any kind),
    destemmed, if necessary,
    and diced
1 chicken thigh, boneless
    and skinless, cut into
    1 cm (½ in) cubes
200 g (7 oz/1¼ cups) cooked rice
    (from about 100 g (3½ oz)
    uncooked; rice that has been
    chilled in the fridge works best)
1 tbsp ketchup
1 tbsp soy sauce
salt and pepper, to taste

FOR THE OMELETTE

3 eggs, beaten with a generous
    pinch of salt
15 g (½ oz) butter

Japanese onomatopoeias are so expressive that sometimes I feel like you can get a sense for what they mean even if you don't speak Japanese. For example, *neba-neba* is the word used for the distinct sliminess of okra or natto, and *puri-puri* describes the bouncy snap of a prawn (shrimp) or a sausage. There are several words for different kinds of crunchiness: *kari-kari* for coarse, hard foods like fried noodles; *pari-pari* for things with a softer crunch, like crispy chicken skin; and for super-light crispy foods like tempura, *saku-saku*, which can also be used to describe the sound of rustling leaves.

For omurice – the Japanese comfort food classic of fried rice topped with an omelette – the key words are *fuwa-fuwa* (fluffy and light) and *toro-toro* (creamy and rich); these are often combined as *fuwa-toro*, a word that neatly describes the Holy Grail of omelette textures: fluffy on the outside, soft and runny in the middle. The best omurice restaurants in Japan make wonderful theatre out of this technique, tipping the wobbly omelette out of the pan and onto the rice directly in front of the customer, then slicing down the centre of the omelette with a sharp knife, so that it falls open, blanketing the rice and exposing the luscious, soft-set scrambled egg within. To have a look at this technique in astonishing action, Google Motokichi Yukimura, the charming chef-owner-showman of restaurant Kichi Kichi in Kyoto, and perhaps the world's only omurice celebrity.

This technique takes serious practise, but do not be discouraged if you don't get it right, because you'll still be able to eat tasty eggs on delicious rice.

You will need a very reliable non-stick pan for this – do not attempt without one.

(Cont. overleaf)

METHOD

To make the sauce, combine the port, stock and tomato purée in a small saucepan and bring to the boil over a high heat. Reduce to the consistency of a thin syrup, then stir in the ketchup, soy sauce and Worcestershire sauce and simmer for 2–3 minutes. Remove from the heat and whisk in the butter.

To make the rice, melt the butter in a frying pan (skillet) over a medium–high heat, add the shallot or onion and sauté until translucent, about 4–5 minutes. Add the mushrooms and chicken and continue to sauté for another 4–5 minutes until the chicken is cooked through. Add the rice, breaking up any clumps, and stir in the ketchup and soy sauce. Taste and adjust the seasoning, as needed, with salt and pepper.

Keep the sauce and the rice warm while you prepare the omelette. Beat the eggs well with the salt, then pass through a sieve – you need the egg to be totally smooth to form a smooth, structurally sound omelette that won't break. Heat the butter in a non-stick frying pan over medium–low heat; when the pan feels hot when you hold your hand over its surface, tip in the beaten eggs and immediately begin to scramble them with chopsticks, whisking through the centre of the pan in a figure-of-eight motion.

After a few minutes of scrambling, your chopsticks will begin to leave trails through the eggs; this means that they have set on the bottom, but should remain runny on top. At this point, tip the pan away from you, tilting the far side of the pan downwards, and use a flexible spatula to gently coax the near side of the omelette onto itself. We often think of 'folding' omelettes, but in this case you want to roll it up, like a carpet, using gravity and the contours of the pan to assist you. Continue to gently push the omelette away from you until it settles into a kind of floppy mass at the far side of the pan.

Now, go in with your spatula underneath the omelette from the opposite side to tease it away from the far side of the pan and ensure the bottom is completely loose and free. Here comes the tricky part: you need to 'bounce' the pan so that the omelette flips over, towards you, so that the runny top slides underneath the cooked bottom, and the omelette cooks and seals all around. Imagine the egg is like a wave, cresting, curling up, and then gently crashing towards you on the shore. To do this, you need to hold the pan handle at the tip, then bash your wrist with your other hand to make the pan jump up and down, controlling the movement of the egg with a subtle back-and-forth movement as you do this. If you are struggling to 'bounce' the omelette over itself, you can very gently flop it over using your spatula; just remember to use the edge of the pan to your advantage. Don't rush, but work quickly, so the liquid centre doesn't cook and set as you're struggling to flip it – you may want to remove the pan from the heat as you do this so you can take your time. The ideal shape is an oblong 'pouch', like a handbag made of eggs that's also filled with eggs, but something more like a rolled-up crêpe or semicircular envelope will work, too. And I have to reiterate: if this is not working for you, don't worry! Omurice doesn't need to be fancy to be delicious. This is just a bit of fun.

Once your omelette is flipped over, remove it from the heat. Pack the rice into a bowl, then invert it onto a plate. Tip the omelette out of the pan upside-down on top of the rice, then slice it open and pour over the sauce. If you have pulled off the *fuwa-toro* texture, give yourself a massive round of applause – or better yet, demand that your family or guests give you a massive round of applause.

MEAL FOR TWO WITH	PAIR WITH
This is hard to make, so serve it with something simple, like blanched vegetables or a salad!	Red wine or a fizzy drink (soda pop). Or whatever you like to drink when you're rewarding yourself!

CRAB AND SMOKED HADDOCK OMELETTE RICE

スモークハドックの天津飯　　SUMŌKU HADOKKU NO TENSHINHAN

A popular variant of omurice is *tenshinhan*, a Chinese-Japanese dish consisting of a crab omelette served on rice with a tangy, starch-thickened sauce called *ankake*. Though they aren't really similar in terms of specific flavours, this dish has always reminded me of the British classic omelette Arnold Bennett, also a seafood omelette in a rich sauce, though the seafood is typically smoked haddock, and the sauce is full of cream and butter. This recipe is more or less a classic tenshinhan, but I have included some smoked haddock, which I've always felt works really well in Japanese food, echoing the smoky fish flavour of dashi.

METHOD

Place the haddock in a saucepan with the dashi or stock and bring to a low simmer. Remove the fish with a slotted spoon, then break into flakes and set aside. Heat the oil in a non-stick frying pan (skillet) or well-seasoned wok over a medium–high heat and add the leek. Cook for 4–5 minutes until softened, then add the mushrooms, bamboo and garlic. Continue to cook for 2–3 minutes until the mushrooms and garlic have softened, then remove from the heat, stir in the crab meat and flaked haddock, transfer to a plate and leave to cool. Wipe out the pan with paper towels. Bring the dashi or stock to a simmer and add the soy sauce, vinegar, sake and sugar. Whisk in the cornflour slurry and boil for a few minutes to thicken, then stir in the sesame oil. Taste and adjust seasoning with salt and/or MSG, as necessary.

Beat the eggs with some pepper and a little bit of salt and/or MSG, along with the cooled stir-fried fish and veg. Melt the butter in the frying pan over a medium heat, then tip in the egg mixture. Scramble the eggs for 1–2 minutes, then leave to set on the bottom – keep the top loose. Pile the rice onto a large serving plate or bowl, then drape the omelette over the eggs, and pour over the sauce. Garnish with the peas, if using.

SERVES 2, OR UP TO 4 AS PART OF LARGER MEAL

80 g (3 oz) smoked haddock (undyed if you can)
200 ml (7 fl oz/scant 1 cup) dashi or chicken stock, or a mix of both – instant dashi/stock is best
1 tbsp oil
5 cm (2 in) piece of leek (white part), thinly sliced at an angle
2 shiitake mushrooms, destemmed and thinly sliced
20–25 g (1 oz) bamboo shoots, julienned
1 garlic clove, finely chopped
100 g (3½ oz) white crab meat
1 tbsp soy sauce
1 tbsp vinegar
1 tbsp sake
1 tbsp sugar
1½ tbsp cornflour, mixed with a little water to form a paste
½ tsp sesame oil
salt and/or MSG, to taste
4 eggs
a few pinches of white pepper
1 large knob of butter
200 g (7 oz) rice, cooked according to the instructions on page 219
a spoonful of peas (optional), blanched or briefly microwaved

MEAL FOR TWO WITH
Another Chinese-inspired dish like Glass Noodle and Cucumber Salad (page 38).

PAIR WITH
Oolong tea.

This chapter is pretty short, because desserts aren't much of a thing in izakaya. In fact, they're not much of a thing in Japanese meals generally; they usually end with a savoury course, or perhaps with some fresh fruit or a simple sorbet. Sweets are more commonly enjoyed on their own, usually with tea or coffee.

デザート

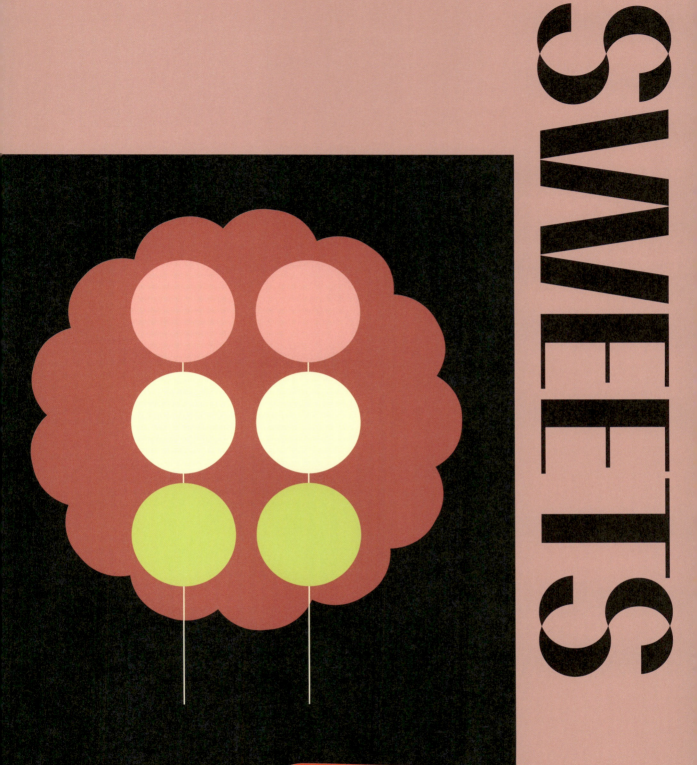

SWEETS

NO-CHURN BANANA, BROWN SUGAR AND MISO SORBET

味噌と黒糖のバナナソルベ
MISO TO KOKUTŌ
NO BANANA SORUBE

I have always found bananas to have a wonderful affinity with miso, which contains a range of complementary aromas like caramel, malt, nuts and ripe fruit. And, of course, miso is salty, which enhances bananas' natural sweetness, and it also lowers their freezing point slightly, which helps prevent this sorbet from becoming over-hard and crystallised. You can adjust the amount of miso to your liking here; the quantity indicated will give you a subtle but noticeable twang; add a bit more if you want this to be more boldly salty-funky.

SERVES 2–4

4 ripe bananas, thinly sliced
4 tbsp brown sugar (any kind will do,
    but I like coconut sugar for this)
2 tbsp red miso

METHOD

Toss the banana slices in a bowl with the brown sugar so that it dissolves and forms a glaze. Tip the bananas out onto a tray lined with baking parchment and spread them out in a single layer. Try not to let them touch each other, but it'll be fine if a few of them do. Transfer to the freezer and freeze completely – probably about four hours minimum. Place the frozen bananas in a food processor with the miso and blitz until completely smooth, then serve immediately, or transfer to a container and re-freeze. Allow the ice cream to come to room temperature for 10–15 minutes before serving.

PAIR WITH
Dark rum, coffee or strong roasted green tea.

YUZU AND SHŌCHŪ ICE WITH CANDIED SATSUMAS

みかんのシロップ漬けと柚子と焼酎のグラニテ
MIKAN NO SHIROPPU ZUKE TO YUZU
TO SHŌCHŪ NO GURANITE

Sometimes, dessert is for delivering that final blow of satiety, something weighty to tamp down the contents of your stomach and get you to a belt-loosening level of fullness. But in Japanese meals, that's kind of what rice and noodles are for, so at the end, if there's any sweet course served at all, it tends to be small, light and refreshing. Sorbets and granitas are common, often showcasing the choicest fruit of the season. For me, it doesn't get much more refreshing than citrus, especially yuzu – and the added booziness of shōchū (page 208) makes this the perfect little frozen digestif dessert.

SERVES 2

1 satsuma, peeled and segmented, with peel reserved
80 ml (2¾ fl oz/⅓ cup) water
100 g (3½ oz) sugar
4 tbsp yuzu juice
25 ml (scant 2 tbsp) shōchū (rice or barley shōchū
    is best for this)

METHOD

Combine the satsuma peel, water and sugar in a saucepan and bring to the boil. Add the satsuma segments and poach for 5 minutes, then remove with a slotted spoon and transfer to the fridge to chill. Remove the syrup from heat, then leave to infuse for 20–30 minutes. Remove the satsuma peel and add the yuzu juice and shōchū. Pour into a shallow container and transfer to the freezer. After about an hour, it should be semi-frozen; use a fork to scrape and stir the mixture. Check the granita again every 30 minutes, repeating the scraping until the whole thing is frozen solid and has a texture somewhere between a sorbet and a granita. Serve in frozen glasses, topped with the candied satsuma.

PAIR WITH
This is like a drink, so it doesn't need a drink to go with it. A little bit more shōchū wouldn't be a bad choice, though.

SWEET POTATO MONT BLANC

さつまいものモンブラン　SATSUMA IMO NO MON BURAN

The Mont Blanc is a pastry that has been so enthusiastically adopted in Japan, it may as well be Japanese – in fact I would wager there are more places, per capita, to get Mont Blancs in Tokyo than there are in Paris. I attribute this to the general popularity of French patisserie in Japan combined with Japan's own tradition of chestnut sweets. Most Mont Blancs in Japan are quite true to the French originals, but sometimes they are made with different Japanese ingredients instead of or in addition to chestnuts. Sweet potatoes work particularly well, I think, because they have such a similar flavour and texture to chestnuts and as a bonus, they add a striking visual element if you buy purple or orange ones.

METHOD

Preheat the oven to 200ºC (400°F/gas 7). Wash the potato to remove any dirt, then wrap in foil and place in the oven. Bake for 40 minutes–1 hour until the potato is soft throughout. Remove and transfer to the fridge to chill completely. Unwrap the potato and remove the skin. Cut four 2.5 cm (1 in) chunks of potato and set aside, and mash the remaining potato through a sieve to make a smooth purée. Whip the cream together with the sugar, vanilla and liquor, if using, to soft peaks. Place a biscuit on top of each meringue nest, then top each biscuit with a potato chunk. Dollop the whipped cream in a large mound on top of the potato chunk, covering the entire surface of the meringue as well. If you have a potato ricer, transfer the potato purée to this and use it to squeeze strands of potato onto the top of each Mont Blanc. Alternatively, you can use a piping bag fitted with a very narrow nozzle to do this. If you don't have a ricer or a piping bag, just do your best to dollop the potato purée on top of the cream. These can be made a few hours in advance and kept in the fridge until ready to serve.

PAIR WITH
Shōchū, dark rum or strong roasted green tea.

SERVES 4

300 g (10½ oz) sweet potato (purple is best)
200 ml (7 fl oz/scant 1 cup) double (heavy) cream
1 tbsp icing (confectioner's) sugar
seeds of 1 vanilla bean, or 1 tsp vanilla paste
1 tsp brandy or dark rum (optional)
4 small meringue nests
4 round shortbread biscuits (the pecan and toffee biscuits from M&S are very good for this)

TIP

For whatever reason, some orange sweet potatoes are often quite watery after roasting. If this is the case, after you have sieved your potatoes, cook the purée in a pan over a medium–low heat for about 8 minutes, stirring constantly, to dry them out.

MOCHI WITH TOASTED SOY FLOUR AND BROWN SUGAR SYRUP

黒蜜きな粉餅   KUROMITSU KINAKO MOCHI

Japanese food is full of extraordinarily simple yet delicious flavour combinations, and that extends to sweets as well. One of the most classic and delicious of these combos is *kuromitsu* and *kinako*: black sugar syrup and toasted soy flour. Kuromitsu is made from *kokutō*, or black sugar – not actually black, of course, but very dark brown, with a rich aroma of liquorice and dried fruits. Kinako is simply dried soybeans, toasted until nutty, then ground to a powder. It tastes a bit like peanut butter. This combination is most commonly found on *warabi mochi*, a jelly-like sweet made from the starch of Japanese ferns, but it's also used on ordinary rice *mochi*, as well, which is what this recipe is for.

METHOD

Heat the oven to 180ºC (350ºF/gas 6). Bake the soybeans in a roasting tin for aout 10–15 minutes until brown in colour and nutty in aroma. Leave to cool, then blitz to a fine powder in a spice mill or food processor. Combine the rice flour and icing sugar in a heatproof bowl. Add a third of the water and stir to combine, add another third and stir again, then add the remaining water and stir until the mixture is smooth and glossy. Cover the bowl in cling film (plastic wrap) and microwave for 2 minutes, then stir the mixture, re-cover, and microwave for another 2 minutes; it should be solid and opaque and have a consistency similar to melted mozzarella. If not, stir again, and keep microwaving at 30-second intervals until done. Remove the mochi from the bowl and dust with cornflour and icing sugar, and leave to cool to room temperature. Combine the sugar and water and stir until the sugar dissolves completely, then leave this to cool, as well. When the mochi is cool, divide into eight equal portions and roll each portion into a little ball. To serve, cover the mochi with kinako and pour over the kuromitsu. Keep these covered at room temperature and eat them within a few hours.

SERVES 2

20 g (¾ oz) dried soybeans
150 g (5 oz/scant 1¼ cups) glutinous rice flour
4 tbsp icing (confectioner's) sugar, sifted, plus more, for dusting
150 ml (5 fl oz/scant ⅔ cup) water
cornflour (cornstarch), for dusting
4 tbsp very dark brown sugar, such as Japanese *kokutō*, dark muscovado or molasses sugar
1½ tbsp boiling water

TIP

You don't have to make your own kinako for this, but you might not be able to get pre-made kinako, and besides, making your own is way cheaper. If you prefer to use store-bought kinako that is absolutely okay.

PAIR WITH
Matcha.

SAKE GLASS JELLY WITH SEASONAL FRUIT

旬の果物と日本酒ゼリ   SHUN NO KUDAMONO TO NIHONSHU ZERĪ

Good sake often has ebullient fruity notes, ranging from crisp green apple-y acidity to overripe melon-y musk. This makes it a perfect pairing for actual fruit, and often in Japan, top-quality seasonal fruits are carefully selected and prepared, then preserved within a clear, glass-like sake jelly. They're as refreshing as they are pretty.

METHOD

How to prep your fruit will depend on what kind you're using, and how big your moulds are. If your moulds are big enough, you can put half a peach, uncut, in each one. Berries don't need anything done to them, unless you happen to have some particularly unwieldy strawberries. Big fruits like melons and pineapples should be very ripe and diced into slightly smaller than bize-size pieces. Pears should be peeled. Don't use anything hard, like apples. It's also best to avoid anything too sour. The whole idea is that the fruit and the sake sort of become one, texturally and in terms of flavour.

Soak the gelatine in a bowl of cold water. Bring the sake to a boil in a saucepan, and cook for 4–5 minutes to boil off the alcohol. Remove from heat, then add the sugar and stir to dissolve. Taste the liquid and add more sugar as needed – you don't want this *too* sweet, just enough to enhance the sake and the fruit. When the sake is sweetened to your liking, bring back to a very low simmer. Squeeze any excess water out from the soaked gelatine leaves and stir them into the hot sake, then remove from heat. Pour a little bit of the mixture into four to six flexible plastic dishes, cups or pudding moulds, so it comes up to a depth of about 5 mm (¼ in). Transfer to the fridge and leave to chill and set – it should take about an hour. Divide the fruit evenly into each mould and pour over the remaining sake, then transfer to the fridge again to set completely. This will probably take about 4 hours, but it's better to let them set overnight. To serve, gently warm the moulds by dipping them briefly in a bowl of hot water, overturn the containers onto small plates and squeeze them. The jellies should release from their moulds and slide out. Enjoy while still fridge-cold.

SERVES 4–6

about 250–300 g (9–10½ oz) top-quality seasonal fruit, prepared (see method, opposite), plus a little more, to garnish
4 leaves of gelatine
400 ml (13 fl oz/generous 1½ cups) fruity sake (likely, but not necessarily, a 'premium' sake – see page 204)
6 tbsp sugar, or slightly more or less, to taste

PAIR WITH
Umeshu or matcha.

MATCHA, VANILLA AND STRAWBERRY CHEESECAKE PARFAIT

シメパフェ **SHIME PAFE**

Sapporo is a fabulous city in the north of Japan, known for beer, grilled lamb and dairy products – especially cheese and ice cream. It is, as you might expect, one of the greatest drinking towns on the planet, coincidentally located along the same latitude as Milwaukee, another city famously fuelled by beer and cheese. The dairy culture is so pervasive in Sapporo that instead of a typical savoury shime to finish off an izakaya meal or a night of drinking, many locals will instead opt for a 'shime parfait,' essentially a large, late-night ice cream sundae that serves the same sort of satiating purpose as a bowl of ramen. This particular parfait showcases the delicious combination of matcha, vanilla and strawberry, providing a lovely interplay of sweet, bitter, sharp and creamy.

METHOD

Whisk together the matcha, 1 tablespoon of the icing sugar and 2 tablespoon of the cream until smooth, then pass through a small, fine sieve to remove any lumps. Combine the remaining cream and sugar with the cream cheese and vanilla and beat together until light and fluffy. Fold the jam and two of the biscuits through the cream cheese mixture. Layer the ice cream, cream cheese mixture, matcha cream, strawberries and remaining biscuits into tall sundae glasses or cocktail glasses, finishing with a dollop of cream cheese and a garnish of strawberries.

SERVES 2

1 tsp matcha
2 tbsp icing (confectioner's) sugar
100 ml (3½ fl oz/scant ½ cup) single (light) cream
80 g (3 oz) cream cheese
seeds of 1 vanilla bean, or 1 tsp vanilla paste
2 tbsp strawberry jam
4 digestive biscuits (Graham crackers), crushed
500 ml (17 fl oz/2 cups) vanilla ice cream
5–6 fresh strawberries, destemmed and halved

PAIR WITH

If you have reached the point in the evening where you are eating a ridiculous, over-the-top sundae, it might be time to stop drinking.

It's just not an izakaya without drinks; in fact, it's not an izakaya *by definition*. You need drinks! So let's get some. This chapter provides a general guide on what to buy to stock your home izakaya bar, and how to serve them.

飲み物

DRINKS

SAKE

They say food and sake do not fight; I absolutely agree. Unlike beer or wine, sake doesn't have extreme bitter or acidic flavours, which makes it an easy-going sidekick for pretty much everything. Of course, there are cases where sake is not the best choice – spicy foods are a challenge – but if you're looking for just one thing to have at the table that will work with a wide variety of dishes, sake is easily the most versatile option.

This section is adapted from my second book, *JapanEasy*. Apologies if you already own *JapanEasy*, but I have to assume the reader has no prior knowledge of sake. Besides, the best way to expand your sake knowledge isn't by reading more about it, it's by drinking more of it! Keep trying new sake, and take note of each one's unique characteristics. Over time, you'll land on a few favourites – but never stop exploring the boundless world of Japan's national beverage.

If you're just getting acquainted with sake, a good place to start is by getting a few different varieties. I would recommend getting a bottle of **cheap sake**, a bottle of **premium sake** and a bottle of **special sake**. I'll explain these on the next page, but first, some basics: sake rice is polished before brewing, a process in which proteins and other compounds from the outside of the rice grain are buffed away to expose the pure starch at the centre of the grain, which ferments more cleanly and yields a different (and generally more favourable) flavour profile. This process determines the grade of sake, but there is another, overlapping categorisation based on whether or not distilled alcohol has been added that also influences flavour, price and perceived quality. This alcohol sometimes serves to fortify and heighten aroma, so there are actually premium sake with added alcohol, but more often it's added simply to increase yields. Enter our old friend, the cheap stuff.

CHEAP SAKE

Cheap sake, or more flatteringly, table sake or normal sake (*futsū-shu* in Japanese) is made from rice that's not been polished to any notable degree, and has added alcohol. It tends to be rougher around the edges with a pronounced alcoholic heat, and the use of less polished rice yields strong, earthy flavours. It is not usually very acidic, and it can range from kinda sweet to extremely dry. Try a few, and if you discover one you like, then you're in luck! Make a note of the brewer and try to seek out other sake they produce. And if you don't find any cheap sake you like, no worries. Let's move on to the premium stuff.

PREMIUM SAKE

Premium-grade sake is defined by falling into any of the following three categories:

Junmai, or 'pure rice': sake that does not have any added alcohol and has been made from rice polished to a minimum 70% of its original weight

Ginjō: sake made from rice that has been polished to 60% of its original weight

Daiginjō: sake made from rice that has been polished to 50% of its original weight

Junmai is where you will generally start to notice a difference in aroma compared to table sake. With more pure starch exposed in the rice, and without any distilled alcohol, junmai tend to be smoother, fruitier, and a bit more delicate. *Ginjō* and *daiginjō* are often junmai as well, but sometimes they are made with a small amount of added alcohol. Either way, their flavours are clean, refined, and complex. They are often exuberantly fruity, yet delicate and subtle. However, the yeast used in fermenting sake plays a huge role in its flavour profile as well; two sake that are brewed identically but fermented with different yeast strains can have very different aromas. Many breweries use locally cultivated, proprietary yeasts that give their sake distinctive flavours and real terroir. So even within the same category or region, there is a wonderful range of flavours to be found.

SPECIAL SAKE

In addition to designations applied to premium sake, there are a variety of other special categories or descriptors to look out for when choosing sake, especially if you've tried a fair amount of basic sake and are looking for new, exciting flavours.

Nigori: Sake that has been very loosely filtered, leaving a large amount of rice sediment in the finished product. It is milky white, smooth, and often sweet, but with a yoghurt-like tang.

Kimoto and yamahai: Sake in which very old-school production methods are used to allow wild yeasts and bacteria to develop in the sake, producing funky, tart, earthy flavours. Think of these as like the sourdough of sake.

Genshu: Undiluted sake. Higher alcohol content (upwards of 18–20%) tends to boost aroma and make the sake feel more sharp on the palate, even if it's not very dry.

Taruzake: Sake that has been matured in Japanese cedar casks. It has an evocative, rich, peppery, woodsy flavour that works well with rich and spicy food, and is great to enjoy warm.

Koshu: Aged sake. These are rare but often really, really delicious, calling to mind fine sherries or dessert wines.

Sparkling sake: Sake with bubbles. Some of these are sweet and weak, like sake shandies, while others are lush and robust like vintage champagnes or Belgian saisons.

SERVING SAKE

So you've got yourself some sake. Now it's time to drink it! First of all, I would not recommend drinking any sake warm or hot unless specifically recommended by the brewer. Hot sake can be lovely if it's the right kind, but most sake are better chilled or perhaps at room temperature. When you heat up sake, everything becomes more volatile; in premium sake, this means that more delicate fruity and floral aromas are lost, and in cheap or very dry sake, it brings the raw, boozy heat of alcohol to the fore. Subtle, savoury sake with robust, earthy aromas tend to work well warmed up, but as a general rule, get your sake in the fridge.

Another fun part of drinking sake is the gear. If I've got a special sake, I usually drink it in white wine glasses, which are a good shape and size for appreciating the flavour, aroma and clarity of premium sake. The problem is, wine glasses are boring. Drinking sake out of nice Japanese sake ware is, I think, all part of the experience. For a proper home izakaya, on the following pages are a few pieces of sake kit you might want to buy:

Ochoko: These are the classic little sake cups, with straight sides and a bowl-like shape. Many izakaya in Japan will have a wide range of mismatched *ochoko*, allowing customers to choose one that suits them. I have always loved this practice, especially because it makes it okay for me to have a bunch of sake ware that doesn't go together. Ochoko are essential for the ritual of pouring sake for one another at the table, a symbol of deference and generosity.

Guinomi: *Guinomi* are similar to ochoko, but a bit larger and more rounded. They're nice for rougher styles, as they tend to make sake feel softer and smoother on the palate. I like guinomi because they hold more sake and I'm greedy.

Masu: These are the iconic square sake cups, made from wood, lacquer or plastic. These are among of my favourite sake vessels, but they come with some caveats. First of all, there's little point to drinking from the ones that aren't made of wood; it's awkward to sip from a square, and it doesn't really do much for the sake. And as for the ones that are made of wood, make sure you get ones that are made from actual Japanese cypress or cedar (*hinoki* or *sugi*, respectively), which are the only ones that provide that lovely 'Japanese bath' aroma. Of course, this aroma can overwhelm more delicate, premium sake, so only use your masu for robust sake that can stand up to it, or for plonk sake that doesn't taste that great in the first place. You can also use masu of any material for one of my favourite sake rituals, the overflowing pour. This is where you set a tall, narrow glass inside a larger masu, then pour the sake into the glass until it overflows into the masu below. This is a symbol of abundant generosity and a lovely bit of theatre.

Tokkuri: *Tokkuri* are the little flasks in which sake is served. They help sake keep its temperature and facilitate pouring; it's kind of tricky to pour sake into tiny glasses directly from the bottle. Tokkuri are also key if you're having hot sake.

There are many ways to heat sake, but probably the easiest is to take a flask of room-temperature sake and place it in a saucepan of just-boiled water for a few minutes. As a general rule, you'll want to get the sake to the temperature of a hot bath – about 40–45°C (75–110°F), but if it's really chilly outside and you've got a sake that can withstand high heat, you can push it up to around 50°C (120°F).

Truly though, what's important about sake is that it's fun. You don't need to be a connoisseur to enjoy it – despite everything I've said, just find one you like, serve it at the temperature you like, in whatever vessel you like, with food and people you like, and that's all you really need.

SHŌCHŪ

Shōchū is Japan's distilled spirit – a delicious and diverse beverage that can be made from pretty much anything, but most commonly rice, barley or sweet potatoes. It is sometimes described as a kind of Japanese vodka, but that isn't quite right. For one thing, shōchū is typically distilled only once, which means it is usually significantly weaker than most spirits (around 25% alcohol) and also carries more flavour from the base ingredient it's fermented from. Just like sake, it can be earthy, nutty and rich, or light, fresh and fruity, and everything in between. Because shōchū's flavours can vary so widely, it can be a bit difficult to know where begin, but here is a general guide I use when recommending shōchū to customers at the restaurant:

If you like **vodka**, try a **rice shōchū**, which are typically clean, smooth and slightly sweet.

If you like **rum**, try a **barley shōchū**, especially an aged one if you can, as these tend to have subtle flavours of caramel, vanilla and nuts.

If you like **tequila**, try **buckwheat shōchū**, which have a similar kind of earthy, floral flavour.

If you like **whisky**, I recommend **sweet potato shōchū**, which are rich and full-flavoured, with nutty, fruity and sometimes even smoky notes.

Shōchū can be enjoyed in many ways, most commonly neat, on the rocks, cut with an equal measure of hot or cold water or in the delicious dry cocktail chūhai (page 213). In general, with food, I have it on the rocks, as it smooths out some of the rougher edges. Shōchū is sometimes confused with *soju*, a Korean rice spirit that's similar in some ways, but markedly different in others. But soju is tasty, too, and some izakaya do stock it; it would be ideal with some of the Korean dishes in this book, like Korean-style Beef Tartare (page 80).

UMESHU AND
OTHER LIQUEURS

Even if you don't tend to go for fruity booze, I would strongly encourage
you to try umeshu (plum wine) or other Japanese fruit liqueurs. Like sake,
these come in various grades, but unlike sake, really good ones are not
that expensive because they are typically lower in alcohol. These liqueurs
are great well chilled; umeshu, in particular, is lovely on the rocks or with
soda (the latter is especially nice in the summertime). Similar liqueurs may
be made with fruits such as yuzu, nashi pears or Japanese apricots – many
of these are absolutely gorgeous, as lush and aromatic as any Sauternes.

Even though sake is the official national beverage of Japan, in actuality, beer reigns supreme, and there's no doubt that's partly due to its compatibility with Japanese food. Of course, Japanese beer tends to be light, dry, fizzy rice lagers, and their clean, bland flavour makes them easy to drink and food-friendly. Pale lagers just work, and beers with a strong hop presence often clash with Japanese dishes, so if you want to drink something a bit nicer than Asahi, generally speaking I'd stay within the Belgium-Germany- Czech Republic corridor: think pilsners, wheat beers and saisons. These days you can also get a few different Japanese craft beers in the UK, which are very good, and sometimes brewed with distinctly Japanese ingredients or flavours, such as yuzu, ginger and cedarwood.

WHISKY

People have gone so crazy for single-malt Japanese whisky that it's actually become hard to get some of the more well-known brands. But they *are* fabulous, and in my opinion, generally worth their somewhat inflated price tags. (Cheaper Japanese whiskies are now available in the UK as well, but to me, there's not much point to them – they're not particularly distinguishable from Scottish equivalents, but they're still more expensive.) But if you're just having highballs, there's no need to get anything fancy – just bust out the Johnnie Walker. Like fizzy yellow lager or table sake, no-frills whisky highballs like this are great all- rounders when it comes to food: tasty enough to keep you quaffing but not so flavourful that they interfere.

TEA AND SOFT DRINKS

Soft drinks selections at izakaya are generally limited to fruit juice, non-alcoholic beer, cola and perhaps *ramune*, the iconic Japanese lemonade in a marble-sealed glass bottle. These are all decent options, providing the same kind of unobtrusive refreshment that lager or highballs do. But if you want something with a bit more character, look no further than tea. In most casual restaurants in Japan, tea is the default option for soft drinks. There are many, many kinds, but here are a few major ones:

Oolong: While oolong isn't Japanese, it's hugely popular in Japan, and its strong, robust flavour makes it an ideal choice for izakaya dishes.

Ryokucha/sencha: *Ryokucha* means green tea, and sencha indicates that it is whole-leaf tea. Basically, these are catch-all terms for Japanese green tea and you will see both used on labels. There's a wide variety of sub-categories, but generally, Japanese green tea is sharp, grassy and light.

Genmaicha: This is green tea that has toasted brown rice added to it, giving it a rich, slightly sweet, distinctly 'popcorn-y' aroma and flavour.

Hōjicha: Tea that has been roasted until it develops a rich, caramelised flavour, this is very comforting on a crappy day, and versatile with food – a great choice for izakaya.

Barley tea: Not actually a tea, what's called *mugicha* is an infusion of dark-roasted barley grains, with a deliciously nutty, subtly sweet flavour. Like oolong, it's robust enough to work with spicy or strongly flavoured dishes, but its mellow nature also makes it a good all-rounder. It's also a good choice if you're avoiding caffeine.

Matcha: The espresso of green tea: thick and intense, sharp and fresh. It doesn't really work so well with savoury food, and it's awkward for an izakaya setting because it can't be quaffed – but it's lovely with sweets.

All of these teas can be cold-infused, which is how I'd generally recommend serving them with an izakaya meal. Cold brewing eliminates the risk of excessive bitterness, and it makes the tea more refreshing. That said, in the depths of winter there's almost nothing more comforting than a hot drink with a hotpot dinner. It's all about drinking seasonally, and to suit your mood, of course.

COCKTAILS

Cocktail culture is big in Japan, but most izakaya have a fairly limited cocktail menu. These are almost always long drinks, which can be made easily and quickly, and generally work better with food. Highballs are the classic choice: whisky, shōchū or umeshu, sometimes flavoured with fruit or tea, topped up with soda water and lots of ice. The following are a few simple cocktails that you might find on izakaya menus that are versatile partners for food. All recipes yield one serving.

CLASSIC HIGHBALL

ハイボール

HAIBŌRU

Highballs are *the* cocktail at izakaya; in fact, they're often the only one available. They are so classic and so simple they hardly need a recipe. I like highballs to be pretty strong; like any cocktail, they're a statement of intent.

6–8 ice cubes
50 ml (1¾ fl oz/3 tbsp) blended whisky, shōchū or umeshu
90 ml (3 fl oz/⅓ cup) soda water
1 lemon wheel

METHOD

Put the ice in a highball glass and pour in the liquor and soda. Stir to mix, then garnish with the lemon wheel.

CASSIS OOLONG

カシスウーロン

KASHISU ŪRON

Crème de cassis is a pretty niche liqueur here in the UK but it's a perennial favourite in Japan. The combination with oolong tea is a perfect match, bringing an earthy sophistication and light bitterness to offset the syrupy sweetness of the cassis.

6–8 ice cubes
35 ml (2 tbsp) crème de cassis
90 ml (3 fl oz/⅓ cup) chilled oolong tea
    (this can either be cold-infused or brewed hot
    and then chilled; the latter will be stronger and
    a bit more bitter)
1 lemon wheel

METHOD

Put the ice in a highball glass and pour in the cassis and tea. Stir to mix, then garnish with the lemon wheel.

UMESHU KIR

梅酒キール

UMESHU KĪRU

Another popular cassis-based cocktail in Japan is the very old-school Kir, a simple but effective mixture of cassis and wine. This version includes some umeshu as well, which is not typical, but I like the additional acidity and aroma it provides.

15 ml (1 tbsp) chilled crème de cassis
15 ml (1 tbsp) chilled umeshu
90 ml (3 fl oz/⅓ cup) chilled dry white wine

METHOD

Pour everything into a wine glass and enjoy.

SALTED GRAPEFRUIT SHŌCHŪ HIGHBALL

ソルティグレープフルーツチューハイ

SORUTI GURĒPUFURŪTSU CHŪHAI

Often in Japan, shōchū highballs are made with fruit syrups or sometimes freshly pressed fruit juice. Grapefruit is a particularly popular option, though its strong flavour means you shouldn't use any fancy shōchū for this. The combination of salt and citrus works very well, calling to mind a classic Salty Dog.

salt, as needed
6–8 ice cubes
50 ml (1¾ fl oz/3 tbsp) shōchū
3 tbsp freshly squeezed pink grapefruit juice
50 ml (1¾ fl oz/3 tbsp) soda water
1 grapefruit slice

METHOD

Moisten the rim of a highball glass with a slightly damp cloth or paper towel, then line it with the salt. Put the ice in the glass and pour in the liquor, juice and soda along with an additional pinch of salt. Stir to mix, then garnish with the grapefruit slice.

NANHATTAN NO. 2

ナンハッタン　ナンバーツー

NANHATTAN NANBĀ TSŪ

This isn't a cocktail from Japan, but rather from my own izakaya, Nanban, in Brixton. I absolutely love Manhattans and wanted to offer some version of it, so after some tinkering, came up with this new recipe. In truth, it's not really a Manhattan, because it swaps out most of the whiskey for sake, but it still has a similar flavour profile and the same attitude-adjusting effect.

50 ml (1¾ fl oz/3 tbsp) taruzake (cedar-aged sake)
1 tsp dry vermouth (we use Lillet blanc)
1 tsp sweet vermouth (we use Punt e Mes)
2 dashes of orange bitters
2 dashes of Angostura bitters
ice, as needed
½ tsp Bourbon or rye whiskey
1 dark cherry
1 strip of orange peel

METHOD

Shake the taruzake, both vermouths and the bitters with plenty of ice. Rinse a chilled martini glass with the Bourbon. Place the cherry in the glass and strain the cocktail over it. Twist the orange peel over the finished cocktail before serving.

These are some useful sauces, seasonings and condiments that come up repeatedly, not just in this book, but in Japanese cookery in general. Many of them can be purchased pre-made, and they're almost always quite good. But if you can't get them, or just want to learn how to make them yourself, they are quite easy to do.

FUNDAM

料理の基本

MENTALS

HOW TO COOK JAPANESE RICE

Job one for the vast majority of Japanese meals is cooking rice. If you have a rice cooker, you should use that, of course. If not, you'll just need a saucepan with a snug-fitting lid and some scales.

The ratio of rice to water for household quantities of rice is 1 to 1.3 by weight, and you'll need about 100 g (3½ oz) of rice per serving.

Weigh out the rice into a pan. Now, you'll need to wash it. Fill the pan with water, then swish the grains around and massage them gently, then drain the water out and repeat this process three or four times. Drain the washed rice very well, then return to the pan and pour water measured in the correct ratio. Swirl it around a bit so the grains redistribute and settle in an even layer. If you have time, let the rice soak for 15–30 minutes, but don't worry if you don't.

Place the pan on a high heat with the lid off, and bring to the boil. Place the lid on the pan and turn the heat way down to low. Set a timer for 15 minutes, then leave it to steam.

If you have an induction hob, start the rice off on a medium or low heat; high heat on induction is too quick and intense, which makes the rice stick and burn almost immediately. Use caution, and let the water come to the boil slowly, stirring occasionally to make sure the grains aren't catching.

When the timer is up, turn off the heat and fluff the rice with chopsticks or a fork, using a slice-and-fold motion rather than a dig-and-scoop motion. Put the lid back on the pan and wait another 10 minutes so the residual steam continues to soften the grains and loosen the stuck rice from the bottom of the pan. Finally, give the rice another gentle fluffing, serve, and enjoy.

DASHI

出汁

Dashi is one of the most fundamental ingredients of Japanese cooking – it is a stock which is light in body but deep in flavour. It is made from kombu (dried kelp) and usually katsuobushi, shavings of small tuna that have been smoked, fermented and desiccated until they resemble chunks of dark driftwood. This recipe includes dried shiitake mushrooms, too, which are used in vegetarian dashi. It is not common to use them in addition to katsuobushi, but the combination produces what's called 'synergistic umami,' in which different savoury compounds within them amplify each other.

MAKES ABOUT 500 ML (17 FL OZ/2 CUPS)

10 g (½ oz) kombu (about a 10 cm (4 in) square)
2 dried shiitake mushrooms (optional)
600 ml (20 fl oz/2½ cups) water (for really good dashi, it is best to use soft water like Volvic – it will provide a fuller flavour)
15 g (½ oz) katsuobushi

METHOD

Place the kombu and dried mushrooms, if using, in a saucepan and pour in the water. Place the pan on a very low heat – kombu releases its flavour most readily at a temperature range from cold to just below the boiling point, so the more time you keep it in that range, the more flavourful your dashi will be. When the water barely begins to simmer, with just a few small bubbles breaking the surface of the water, add the katsuobushi, remove from the heat, and leave to infuse for an hour to maximise flavour extraction. Pass through a fine sieve and gently squeeze out the ingredients. If you like, save the spent ingredients to make tsukudani and/or furikake (recipes on page 221). Dashi will keep in the fridge for about a week, and it can be frozen, but fresh is best. I would recommend using it immediately, or within a few days.

TSUYU

つゆ

Tsuyu is essentially a concentrated and highly seasoned dashi, which can be used on its own as a sauce, or diluted to make a quick broth. This recipe provides options to make it from either dashi powder, or from real kombu and katsuobushi. The flavour of the latter is a bit fuller, but for most dishes, the instant dashi version is perfectly serviceable.

MAKES 225 ML (8 FL OZ/SCANT 1 CUP) WHEN MADE FROM DASHI POWDER; MAKES 150 ML (5 FL OZ/SCANT $^2/_3$ CUP) WHEN MADE FROM SCRATCH

1 tsp dashi powder or 10 g (½ oz) kombu, 10 g (½ oz) katsuobushi and 50 ml (1¾ fl oz/3 tbsp) water
100 ml (3½ fl oz/scant ½ cup) soy sauce
100 ml (3½ fl oz/scant ½ cup) mirin
50 ml (1¾ fl oz/3 tbsp) sake
1 tbsp brown sugar

METHOD

If you are using real kombu and katsuobushi, place the kombu in a saucepan along with all the other ingredients except the katsuobushi and leave to infuse for 1 hour. Bring the liquid to a low simmer over a medium heat, then remove the kombu and add the katsuobushi. Let the liquid boil, then remove from the heat and leave to infuse for 10 minutes. Pass the tsuyu through a sieve, gently squeezing the liquid out from the katsuobushi. If you like, save the spent ingredients to make tsukudani and/or furikake (recipes opposite).

If you are using dashi powder, simply combine all ingredients in a saucepan and bring to a bare simmer. Stir to ensure the sugar has dissolved.

Tsuyu can be used as is as a dip, or diluted with a little water for a softer flavour. To use as a broth for soup, dilute 75 ml (5 tbsp) tsuyu with 275 ml (9 fl oz/generous 1 cup) water to yield 350 ml (12¼ fl oz/1½ cups) – enough for a bowl of noodles. Tsuyu will keep in the fridge indefinitely, but its flavour will start to taste a bit stale after about a month.

KATSUOBUSHI FURIKAKE

鰹節ふりかけ

If you've made dashi or tsuyu from scratch, don't throw away the katsuobushi and kombu. They'll still have a lot of flavour and can be re-used. One of the easiest and tastiest things to make with spent katsuobushi is *furikake*, a dry seasoning to sprinkle on rice, but it's also good on popcorn or potatoes (page 100).

a few drops sesame oil
spent katsuobushi from making dashi (page 220)
    or tsuyu (page 220), squeezed dry
50 g (2 oz/⅓ cup) white sesame seeds
30 g (1 oz/scant ¼ cup) black sesame seeds
3 tbsp sea salt, lightly crushed
½ tbsp sugar
½ sheet of nori seaweed or 2 tbsp dried wakame seaweed
    or 2 tbsp similar dried seaweed flakes

METHOD

Preheat the oven to 120°C (250°F/gas 1). Line a roasting tin with foil and use a paper towels to lightly grease it with sesame oil. Chop the katsuobushi into small pieces and separate the flakes best you can. Spread them out on the prepared roasting tin, and put them in an oven for about 45 minutes until they're totally dry, then leave to cool. Toast the sesame seeds in a dry frying pan (skillet) over a medium–high heat until brown and very aromatic (even if they are already toasted, toast them again), then tip out into a bowl and immediately stir in the salt and sugar. Leave to cool completely. Meanwhile, snip the nori into very small shreds using scissors, or if you're using wakame, crush it into fine flakes using a pestle and mortar, food processor or spice grinder. Stir the seaweed into the sesame mixture along with the dried katsuobushi. Keep in a jar in the cupboard for up to 3 months.

KOMBU TSUKUDANI

昆布の佃煮

With rehydrated kombu, you can make one of my all-time favourite preserves called *tsukudani*, in which the kombu is braised with lots of soy sauce and sugar until it becomes tender, and reduces down to a jammy consistency. I absolutely love tsukudani – as far as rice toppings go, I prefer it to furikake. The method works well with other ingredients, too; it's not traditional, but I love making it with beet tops. If you can get shiso, or the shiso-flavoured furikake called *yukari*, then some of that stirred in at the end of cooking will add a delightful aroma.

MAKES ENOUGH FOR ABOUT 4 SERVINGS OF RICE

rehydrated kombu from making dashi (page 220)
2 tbsp soy sauce
2 tbsp sugar
1 tbsp sake
1 tsp mirin
1 tsp vinegar
¼ tsp dashi powder (optional)
water, as needed
2 tsp sesame seeds

METHOD

Cut the kombu into strips about 4 cm (1½ in) wide, then julienne these strips into fine shreds. Place in a saucepan along with the soy sauce, sugar, sake, mirin, vinegar, and dashi powder, if using. Add enough water to cover the kombu by about 2.5 cm (1 in) and bring to the boil. Boil for about 30 minutes, topping up the water as needed, then continue to cook without topping up until the liquid reduces to a very thick glaze (lower the heat and stir frequently at this point to prevent it from burning). There should be almost no liquid left in the pan when it's done. Remove from the heat and stir in the sesame. Leave to cool completely before using.

PONZU

ポン酢

Ponzu is a versatile seasoning made from sour citrus and soy sauce. It is used primarily as a dip, but can be used as a marinade, cooking sauce or salad dressing, as well. A two-to-one mixture of soy sauce and citrus juice will make a basic ponzu, but this recipe has a much fuller flavour.

MAKES ABOUT 225 ML (8 FL OZ/SCANT 1 CUP)

5 tbsp lemon, lime or yuzu juice
    (you can use just one, or mix any or all of the three)
5 tbsp soy sauce
2 tbsp water
2 tbsp caster sugar
1 tbsp mirin
1 tsp vinegar
¼ tsp dashi powder (ideally kombu dashi) or MSG

METHOD

Mix everything well until the sugar dissolves. Keep in a jar in the fridge for up to a month (it won't go off, but the flavours will start to fade).

WAFU DRESSING

和風ドレッシング

'Wafū' means 'Japanese-style', and refers to a broad category of soy sauce-based dressings. The onion and ginger help thicken the sauce and provide a deliciously savoury aroma. For a lighter flavour, replace the sesame oil with vegetable oil or olive oil.

MAKES ABOUT 350 ML (12¼ FL OZ/1½ CUPS), ENOUGH FOR AT LEAST 8 SMALL SALADS

¼ small onion or ½ banana shallot
2 cm (¾ in) piece of ginger root, peeled
100 ml (3½ fl oz/scant ½ cup) soy sauce
100 ml (3½ fl oz/scant ½ cup) mirin
100 ml (3½ fl oz/scant ½ cup) rice vinegar
1 tbsp sesame oil
1 tbsp sesame seeds

METHOD

Finely grate the onion and ginger, and combine with all the other ingredients. Stir to combine, then, ideally, let it sit for 1–2 hours for all the flavours to come together. Alternatively, place everything in a blender and purée until the onion and ginger are broken down. Keep in a jar in the fridge for up to a month.

SESAME DRESSING

ごまドレッシング

This recipe calls for Chinese or Japanese-style sesame paste, which is made from toasted sesame seeds, but tahini is okay, too – it will provide a lighter flavour.

MAKES ABOUT 400 ML (13 FL OZ/GENEROUS 1½ CUPS)

4 tbsp sesame seeds
180 g (6½ oz) sesame paste or tahini
150 ml (5 fl oz/scant ⅔ cup) unsweetened soya milk
2 tbsp sesame oil
3 tbsp vinegar
1 tbsp lemon juice
2 tbsp sugar
2 tbsp soy sauce
¼ tsp salt
½ tsp dashi powder

METHOD

Tip the sesame seeds into a frying pan (skillet) and set over a medium–high heat. Cook the sesame seeds, stirring constantly, for about 10 minutes until they are noticeably more aromatic and darker in colour. Remove from the pan and leave to cool. Coarsely grind the sesame in a mortar, food processor or spice mill, then add the remaining ingredients and stir until the sugar dissolves. Keep in the fridge for up to a week.

RAMEN EGGS

味付け卵

Ajitsuke tamago are marinated eggs most commonly used as a topping for ramen, hence their more common English name, 'ramen eggs'. These are a great drinking snack in and of themselves, but they're also a key component of Potato Salad with Ramen Eggs (page 63) and 'Japaniçoise' Salad (page 65), and can be used as an additional topping for rice, noodles or salads.

MAKES 6 EGGS

6 eggs
100 ml (3½ fl oz/scant ½ cup) soy sauce
3 tbsp mirin
2 tbsp dashi
1 tbsp vinegar

METHOD

Ideally, these eggs should be perfectly medium-boiled; to me, this means a completely set white and a yolk that ranges from firm on the outside, fudgy towards the middle, and still liquid right in the very centre. If you have a tried-and-true method to achieve this, by all means, use it. If not, here's mine: prepare a large saucepan full of water and bring it to a rolling boil, then lower in the eggs. I use fridge-temperature, medium eggs, and cook them for 7 minutes exactly. If yours are large, cook them for 7 minutes and 20 seconds; if they're small, cook them for 6½ minutes. If you keep your eggs at room temperature, cook them for about 20 seconds less. When the timer's up, remove the eggs with a slotted spoon, then chill them quickly in cold (ideally iced) water, then peel them and soak them in the soy sauce, mirin, dashi and vinegar for as long as you can – they'll marinate most evenly in a plastic bag, but any container will do, so long as the eggs are submerged. They'll pick up the flavour after about 2 hours, but they'll be way, way better if you leave them overnight.

SHIOZUKE PICKLES

塩漬けの作り方

Pickles are a key component of Japanese meals, and not only that, they're great drinking snacks. Probably the most achievable is shiozuke, or vegetables pickled simply in salt. These are often only lightly fermented, and eaten after a few days, but feel free to let them pickle longer if you like them more sour. There are no measurements in this recipe, so you can make as much or as little as you like.

fresh vegetables – watery veg like Chinese leaf, cucumbers or daikon work well
salt
flavourings, such as kombu, ginger root, yuzu peel or dried chilli (optional)

METHOD

The amount of salt I use is 2% of the weight of the vegetables. Prepare the veg by cutting them into bite-size chunks. Weigh the prepared veg, then weigh out the appropriate amount of salt – so for 500 g (1 lb 2 oz) veg (for example), use 10 g (½ oz) salt. Rub the salt into the vegetables, then leave for 20–30 minutes for the salt to draw out their moisture. Massage the veg and squeeze them, getting as much salty juice out as possible. Leave to sit for another 20–30 minutes and repeat. By now there should be a few spoonfuls of liquid in the bowl. If you like, mix in a few pieces of julienned kombu, sliced ginger root, yuzu peel or a tiny bit of dried chilli; don't use too much of any of these, they should just provide a bit of aroma, not dominate the flavour of the veg. Pack everything into a jar really tightly and pour over any remaining juice. Never seal a jar of pickles or any other ferment tightly; the gas produced by fermentation builds up within the jar and could cause it to explode.

Push the veg down into a jar with all your might, so the juice rises above the surface; it needs to be fully submerged in the brine or it could go mouldy. Once your veg are covered in a good 5 mm (¼ in) of brine, cover the jar. Leave to ferment at room temperature for about three days, then taste it – when it's soured to your liking, it's good to go. Transfer to the fridge, where it will keep for up to 3 months.

QUICK PICKLE BRINE

浅漬けの素

This is a brine for perhaps the easiest Japanese pickles to make, called *asazuke*. Unlike shiozuke or similar ferments, these will be ready to eat within a day, or even in a few hours if you don't need them to be that sour. The brine can also be re-used once after an initial batch of pickles is depleted.

MAKES ABOUT 500 ML (17 FL OZ/2 CUPS)
100 ml (3½ fl oz/scant ½ cup) water
5 g (⅓ oz) kombu
100 g (3½ oz/½ cup) sugar
2 tsp salt
1 very small pinch of dried chilli (hot pepper) flakes
a few shreds of yuzu or satsuma peel
400 ml (13 fl oz/generous 1½ cups) rice vinegar

METHOD

Combine the water, kombu, sugar, salt, chilli and citrus peel in a saucepan and bring to a low simmer. Remove from the heat, stir to dissolve the sugar, then leave to infuse for 15 minutes. Add the rice vinegar and transfer to a jar (don't pass it through a sieve – keep the kombu and everything in there).

All you have to do now is prepare your veg – cucumbers, carrots, daikon, turnips, lotus root – pretty much anything that's nice and crunchy works well. If you want your pickles fast (as in, just an hour or two), slice them into small pieces so they absorb the brine more quickly. If you can wait for your pickles, I'd recommend keeping your veg whole or just cutting them into fairly large chunks. Anyway, if you cut your veg small, the pickles will be ready in 1–2 hours. If you cut them big they'll be ready in 4–8 hours. Either way, they'll keep in the brine for 6 months in the fridge.

EPILOGUE

21 DECEMBER 2020

This year has been tough. As the days have drawn shorter, colder and damper, it's been hard not to feel the despair of mandatory isolation and the persistent fear of an invisible threat. But what remains a consistent source of joy and solace is home cooking, or perhaps more to the point: home dining.

While I cook Japanese food at home often, it is usually quite basic and humdrum – things like grilled fish with rice and vegetables, or simple stir-fries. Making izakaya food, which is a bit more fun and exciting, has made dinner more of a special occasion. It's a little something to look forward to every day. And it turns out I was wrong: you actually can have toddlers in an izakaya, at least in your home izakaya. They're not that different from drunk adults anyway.

I eat Japanese food on a near-daily basis, but it still has the capacity to transport me – and that's because of both fond memories and associations, as well as the sense of endless discovery that learning about Japanese food provides. During the pandemic, it has also become a different form of escapism: an emotional solace from the troubles of the world outside. Of course, this isn't really about the food, but about having quality time with my family. This is something that has sustained me throughout a difficult year, and it's been facilitated by making dinnertime more of an event. Sometimes when you live with people, you don't always share a life with them. You come and go, rushing between work and other obligations, and even when you're all home at the same time, you can be in different parts of the house, doing different things, or just occupying different headspaces. Having a good meal – and not just a good meal, but a *fun* meal – corrals everybody into the same space, physically and mentally. We all have to eat, so we may as well do it together.

RESOURCES

Because this book will be released into many different international markets, it is impractical to recommend particular shops for Japanese ingredients. You can get most of what you need at ordinary supermarkets anyway, but for anything you can't, please try to seek out and support independent businesses, whether online or in real life. I have nothing against big, evil corporations, except that, you know, they're big and evil. Besides, it's hard to run a small business – really hard. Please help them out instead of giving more money to Jeff Bezos or whomever.

If you enjoy this kind of casual, drink-friendly Japanese food, there are a few other cookbooks I would encourage you to seek out: Mark Robinson's *Izakaya: The Japanese Pub Cookbook*, Harris Salat and Tadashi Ono's *Japanese Soul Cooking*, Wataru Yokota's *The Real Japanese Izakaya Cookbook* and Ivan Orkin's *The Gaijin Cookbook*. All of these contain excellent recipes and showcase the depth and diversity of this style of dining. And for more Japanese recipes in general, I absolutely love the books of Reiko Hashimoto, Atsuko Ikeda and Nancy Hachisu.

If you're keen to learn more about Japanese drinks, Stephen Lyman and Chris Bunting's *The Complete Guide to Japanese Drinks* is hard to beat. For sake, in particular, I love Philip Harper's *The Book of Sake*, though it is now out of print.

Finally, I think it is important to understand the culture behind Japanese food, not than just the practicalities of cooking it. The book of essays *Devouring Japan*, edited by Nancy Stalker, is an excellent place to start, as is Eric Rath's anthology *Japanese Foodways, Past and Present*. These are both collections of shorter articles; you can dip in and out of them easily. And last but not least, my Japanese food bible remains Shizuo Tsuji's classic *Japanese Cuisine: A Simple Art*, which is not just a collection of recipes, but a holistic guide to understanding Japanese food from the ground up.

ACKNOWLEDGEMENTS

This book was not my idea; in fact, my last three books were not my idea, either. They were thought up by Kate Pollard at Hardie Grant. I'm really just a hired hand – these are *her* books and I am so thankful to her for giving me the opportunity to write them. She has passed the torch on this particular book to the wonderful Kajal Mistry, whom I have known for a few years now but not yet had the pleasure of working with directly. And it really is a pleasure – I hope to work with Kajal on many more wonderful books!

The other person who really makes these books possible is my agent Holly Arnold, whose dedication, professionalism, cheery demeanour and extremely low tolerance for bullshit makes her genuinely one of the most positive presences in my life. I owe so much to you, Holly, and I am grateful.

I have to thank our stellar creative team as well: Laura Edwards for her wonderfully understated photography; our stylist Tamara Vos for making my food look far prettier than I ever could; Rachel Vere for sourcing such perfect props; and last but not least, Evi O for her fabulous design work. In Evi, I feel like I have found something of a creative soul mate; this is our fourth collaboration, and it's hard for me to imagine working with another designer.

I also owe many, many thanks to the editorial team consisting of Eila Purvis, Wendy Hobson and MiMi Aye, who worked very hard to make sense of a what wound up being a very complicated and verbose manuscript.

Many thanks are also due to my interviewees – Yuki Serikawa, Emiko Pitman, Yumiko Suzuki and Fumio Tanga – for letting me share their stories, and for sharing their wealth of Japanese food knowledge with me so generously.

I also want to acknowledge some other writers who have inspired and informed me throughout the process of writing this book, whether in terms of practical information or how to approach the writing itself: Atsuko Ikeda, MiMi Aye, Anna Sulan Masing, Jonathan Nunn, Nancy Hachisu, Ivan Orkin, Akemi Yokoyama, Morgan Pitelka, Makiko Itoh and Eric Rath.

Last but certainly not least, I have to thank my family, especially my wife Laura, who is always an island of calm in stormy seas. Especially this year, she has kept me from going insane in a very real way. I would also like to thank my cat Baloo and my daughter Tig for being constant sources of happiness and delight.

ABOUT THE AUTHOR

Tim Anderson is the proprietor of the ramen izakaya Nanban, with branches in Brixton and Covent Garden, London. He is also the author of four previous books on Japanese cookery: *Vegan JapanEasy*, *Tokyo Stories*, *JapanEasy* and *Nanban: Japanese Soul Food*. He has been a student and enthusiast of Japanese food for two decades; after studying Japanese food history in college, he moved to Fukuoka Prefecture to further immerse himself in Japan's highly diverse local food culture. Since moving to London, he has turned his lifelong love of Japanese cooking into a career, after winning *MasterChef* in 2011.

Tim currently resides in Lee, Southeast London, with his wife Laura, daughter Tig, and FIV-positive cat Baloo. His favourite Marvel film is *Spider-Man: Into the Spider-Verse*, but his favourite Marvel Cinematic Universe film is *Captain America: Civil War*.

INDEX

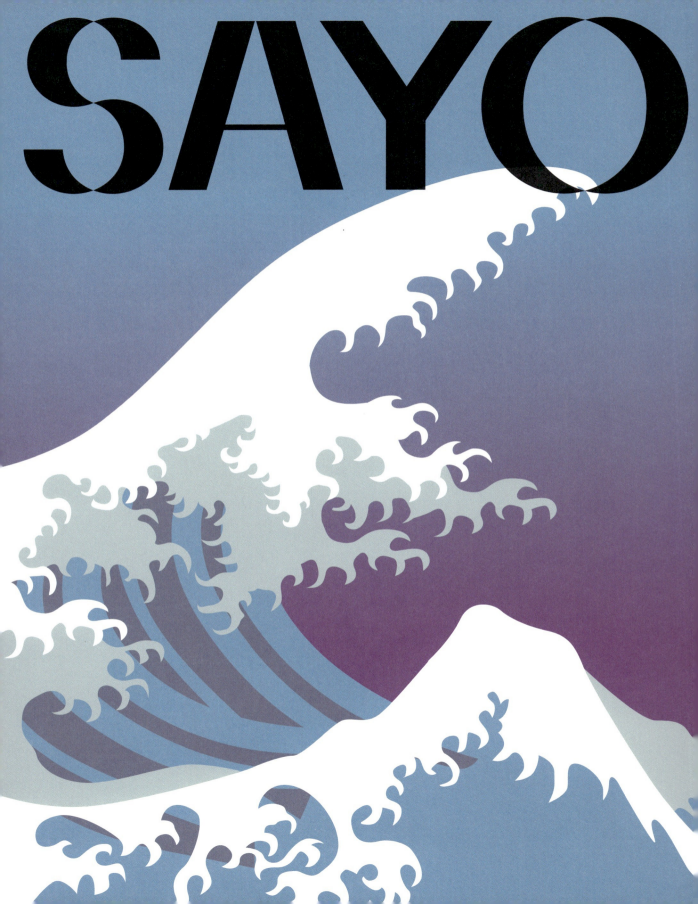

Published in 2021 by Hardie Grant Books,
an imprint of Hardie Grant Publishing

Hardie Grant Books (London)
5th & 6th Floors
52–54 Southwark Street
London SE1 1UN

Hardie Grant Books (Melbourne)
Building 1, 658 Church Street
Richmond, Victoria 3121

hardiegrantbooks.com

British Library Cataloguing-in-Publication Data.
A catalogue record for this book is available from
the British Library.

Your Home Izakaya
ISBN: 978-1-78488-385-0

10 9 8 7 6 5 4

Publisher: Kajal Mistry
Editor: Eila Purvis
Design and Art Direction: Evi-O. Studio | Evi O.
Illustrations: Evi-O. Studio | Evi O. & Susan Le
Photographer: Laura Edwards
Food Stylist: Tamara Vos
Prop Stylist: Rachel Vere
Copy-editor: Wendy Hobson
Proofreader: MiMi Aye
Indexer: Cathy Heath
Production Controller: Katie Jarvis

Colour reproduction by p2d
Printed and bound in China by Leo Paper
Products Ltd.

FSC
www.fsc.org

MIX
Paper from
responsible sources
FSC™ C020056